MW01103793

The Truth About Fiction Writing

The Truth About Fiction Writing

◆

William Appel
Denise Sterrs

HASTINGS HOUSE
Book Publishers
Norwalk, CT

Hastings House
A Division of United Publishing Group Inc.
50 Washington Street
Norwalk, CT 06854

Copyright © 1997 by William Appel & Denise Sterrs

All rights reserved under the International and Pan-American Copyright Conventions. Published in the United States by Hastings House, 50 Washington Street, Norwalk, CT 06854. No part of this publication may be reproduced, stored in a retrieval system, or transmitted in any form or by any means, electronic, mechanical, photocopying, recording or otherwise, without the prior permission of the copyright owners or the publishers.

Library of Congress Catalog Card Number 97-071273

ISBN 0-8038-9390-6

Distributed to the trade by Publishers Group West, Emeryville, CA

Printed in the United States of America

10 9 8 7 6 5 4 3 2 1

I assume from the outset that the would-be writer using this book can become a successful writer if he [or she] wants to, since most of the people I've known who wanted to become writers knowing what it meant, *did* become writers.

—John Gardner in *The Art of Fiction*

CONTENTS

Part I
CRAFT

1

CAN IT BE TAUGHT?

The art of writing fiction cannot be taught, any more than talent or greatness or charisma can.

But craft, technique, method and understanding of the medium can most certainly be taught. So can the proper presentation and marketing of writing.

Please read carefully these words from Thomas McCormack, former chairman and editorial director of St. Martin's Press, in his book *The Fiction Editor*.

> A stipulative definition of craft: It is that part of former art that is now so well understood it has been anatomized and codified, and therefore it can be taught and systematically applied. Perspective in drawing, close-up in film flashbacks and juggled points of view in writing were all

once new, arcane and thus artificial. Today, they're basic elements of craft, routinely part of any studious practitioner's equipment. All craft was once art.

The teaching of craft and technique has long been a tradition in the arts of painting, sculpture, music, dance, acting, etcetera. Even today many visual and performing artists work as apprentices, especially in Europe. Why should writing be any different?

However, there is a strange notion among most lay people and aspiring writers that writing is exclusively an art, in no way reliant on or subordinate to craft or mechanics or acquired skills. Nothing is further from the truth.

Good writing is a perfect indivisible blending and balance of craft and art.

And one way for aspiring writers to improve their craft is through participating in a writer's group. When a group has read and criticized a manuscript, has given the writer opinions on the strengths and weaknesses of that manuscript, the writer stretches and grows to the vision of the group.

He learns his craft, in other words.

Both of us have been members of a writer's group, watching members beam when praised and squirm when panned, always stretching and growing.

We've also taught writing to students through the *Writer's Digest* Correspondence School. We've seen all of our fellow members and students improve as writers. It is impossible to be an ardent member of a serious group of writers who are constantly being exposed to criticism without learning.

> Books on writing tend to make much of how difficult it is to become a successful writer, but the truth is that, though the ability to write well is partly a gift—like the ability to play basketball well, or to analyze the stock market—writing ability is mainly a product of good teaching supported by a deep-down love of writing.
>
> — John Gardner in *The Art of Fiction*

2

THE RIGHT WAY
WITH WORDS

Over the years many students and clients have asked if a formal education is necessary to become a writer. To know that answer all one has to do is read a few of the endless names of writers with little or no education, from Mark Twain to John Cheever and Neil Simon and Louis L'Amour.

A knowledge of grammar is no guarantee that one will write well. If it were, every English teacher, copy editor and editor would be a fine writer.

However, a writer who is very deficient in grammar will find that his flaws—like lack of punctuation—will seriously mar his storytelling. Here a good reference like *Pinckert's Practical Grammar (Writer's Digest Books),* or *Essentials of English* (Barron's), is invaluable.

"Usage is the only test. I prefer a phrase that is easy and unaffected to a phrase that is grammatical."

— W. Somerset Maugham

"Any fool can make a rule and every fool will mind it."

— Henry David Thoreau

"Grammar is a piano I play by ear. All I know about grammar is its power."

—Joan Dideon

These amusing quotes are fun to read. However, in today's demanding market, grammar *does* count. Take it as seriously as editors do, and you'll be fine. Neglect it, and you'll be thought of as an amateur.

3

IT'S NOT A HOBBY

More times than we'd like to remember, people—house-wives, plumbers, cabbies, college professors—have said to us: "I'm going to write a novel as soon as I have the time." As if the only qualifications needed were minutes and hours.

Not long ago we received a phone call from a man who had recently retired. What did we think, he asked, now that Louis L'Amour was dead, about his phoning L'Amour's publisher and offering to write the Sackett series? Was our caller a writer of westerns? No, but he had read every one of L'Amour's novels. Had our caller ever written a novel of any kind? No, but he lived in the western part of the country.

This is an extreme example of a common belief among nonwriters. People just don't say, "I think I'll write a symphony when I have time." They'd consider someone mad who thought he could play the cello without lessons or build a bridge without a master knowledge of engineering. But a novel—that's only a matter of enough time.

After all, doesn't everyone have a story in them?

Everyone does not. What they have are experiences that need to be transformed and pruned and shaped and reshaped to be made into readable, compelling stories.

It is just as rare for someone to make a readable story as it is for someone to make music that's fit for listening or to create a painting suitable for viewing.

People take it for granted that doctors, lawyers, accountants and quarterbacks require long internships before they become professionals. But too many have little respect for what it takes to learn to become a writer.

That's why publishers and agents are constantly bombarded with Everests of manuscripts by people who believe writing is merely jotting down whatever comes to mind. When Truman Capote was asked what he thought of a famous novelist he said, "Typing isn't writing."

Disrespect for writing results in the greatest crime a writer can commit: being a bore.

4

THE PSYCHOLOGICAL BAGGAGE WE BRING TO WRITING

Most beginners want to be writers for the wrong reasons. Many only like the idea of being a writer. They see themselves in safari jackets drinking wine in a Paris cafe, or posing for a book jacket, a cigarette dangling from a corner of their mouths looking as aesthetic as Camus, or autographing copies of their books in B. Daltons.

Fact is, a great number of those who like the idea of being a writer don't like the paperwork. Others write to exorcise their demons, or vent about their pet peeves.

Writers with these and similar reasons for writing are doomed from the outset, because readers don't want to read about an author's problems or likes and dislikes.

Readers read fiction to be entertained. Certainly, they

also enjoy painless learning about, say, what happens behind the scenes in corporate boardrooms or exclusive bordellos, but mainly they read for escape.

Readers do not want to hear a writer's message about ecology or war or how pervasive drugs have become. They have no desire to be a part of a writer's therapy. They want to escape their own world for a more entertaining one. Good writing is not a sermon or a puzzle, or written by superiors for inferiors.

Consider these words from William Sloan in his *The Craft of Writing*:

> The next thing about your reader that's interesting is that he doesn't care at all about you. If he's attending a class or course, he has to care at least nine sentences' worth, which can be stated later in a term paper or on an examination. But the genuine reader doesn't care whether he's reading a book written by a man or a woman, written yesterday or two hundred years ago. Furthermore, he isn't there to be improved by you. He isn't saying, 'Tell me, dear author, about yourself and what you think about the world, art, life, the eternal verities.' What he is saying is so frightening that I urge you not to think about it while you are writing—you may get a kind of palsy. What he is saying is, 'Tell me about me. I want to be more alive. Give me me.' All the great fiction of the world satisfies this need: it tells me about me.

That's what's good about Shakespeare and it's also what's good about Homer. Shakespeare—except when you get hold of a book called *The Doctored Works of Shakespeare* or something of the sort—tells you absolutely nothing about himself. You can't learn anything about Shakespeare in Shakespeare. He, himself, is in dispute among scholars and critics to this very day because all he ever wrote about was you and me. Tell me about me.

Amen.

Most beginners and even some professionals are under the impression that *who* they are has little to do with *what* and *how* they write. This can be no further from the truth.

If a person is a procrastinator, you can bet he'll also delay his writing. If a person thinks the world revolves around him, his writing will be self-centered. Whether a male or female chauvinist, a whiner or a disliker of people, nothing about the person's attitudes will be hidden in his writing.

Nor does it end there: people who are afraid of rejection are poor marketers of their stories and novels.

So what can a writer do? He can accept that the problems he has in the rest of his life will show up in the process of writing. In this way he will not waste time and energy treating any psychological problems he's having with his writing as belonging exclusively to his "writer-self." And in recognizing this, he can anticipate how the chinks in his personality affect his writing, and possibly do something about it.

> I went for years not finishing anything. Because, of course, when you finish something you can be judged . . . I had poems which were rewritten so many times I suspect it was just a way of avoiding sending them out.
>
> — Erica Jong

5

SOME MAJOR REASONS SHORT STORIES AND NOVELS FAIL

A. INCIDENT VERSUS STORY

Basically a story (or novel) is an unfolding of events stemming from a problem and resulting in the resolution of that problem. In other words it's what happens when a character has a problem and overcomes it. The problem or obstacle can be against a villain, like a cruel landlord, or the character's struggle against himself, like an addict trying to give up drugs.

Whatever the problem, the story must move from that problem straight to the resolution. Obstacles to solving the problem build suspense and keep the reader turning pages—but there is a direct journey to a definite destination. That's a story or novel. An incident is an unfolding of an event and—not a thing more. It doesn't go anywhere or make any definite point.

So, a story (or novel) has a definite reason for the unfolding of events. That reason is the solution of the problem planted at the beginning. An incident is the description of an event for the sole purpose of describing it. A story has a predetermined destination. An incident does not. That is why a story is saleable and an incident is not. A story nails the reader to his seat. An incident doesn't hold the reader's interest, because it's merely the telling about something.

Many aspiring fiction writers believe they have a saleable story when they write that a man and a woman met on the job and decided to get married.

This is not in any way a story. It's an incident or anecdote that you might repeat to someone who actually knows that couple, and has a reason for being interested. But to the reader of fiction this incident holds no interest, because there are no obstacles to overcome to raise suspense.

The writer can have a novel, for instance, if a problem arises to keep the man and woman apart. Perhaps it's against the rules of the company for which they work for employees to date. Perhaps their respective families have been at odds for years. The possibilities are endless.

Then, when it appears as if the two will never get together, they do. The reader will breathe a sigh of relief, because he's had the pleasure of worrying about whether these two would indeed become a twosome. In an incident the conclusion is foregone and without strife or conflict, so the vicarious thrill of worrying about the man and woman is missing.

The essential point here is that the intended story is merely an incident if there is not a significant problem plus a bitter struggle to overcome it and an eventual victory.

A story without a problem or obstacle or conflict is only an incident.

B. SLICE OF LIFE WRITING

No other publication has done so much to promote this nontraditional kind of story as the *New Yorker*.

There is no question that a master of style like John Updike need not always have a story and plot in his stories to entertain. But far too few of us can replace these traditional storytelling aids with the brilliant lyricism of an Updike.

One must have learned the traditional means of storytelling before attempting to keep the reader absorbed with nontraditional techniques. As a young man Picasso learned to draw people with a photographer's accuracy. Only then did he begin to draw his subjects abstractly as he saw their personalities.

> "It's not wise to violate the rules until you know how to observe them."
>
> — T.S. Eliot

> "Writing has laws of perspective, of light and shade, just as painting does, or music. If you are

born knowing them, fine. If not, learn them. Then rearrange the rules to suit yourself."

— Truman Capote

C. LACK OF CHANGE IN MAIN CHARACTER AT END

A main character does not have to change at the end to have a story work, but the chances of a story working are greatly increased if he or she does. Actually, almost everything changes in the process of progression and action that is a story—and most especially in a novel. Characters change, relationships change, conflicts change. In fact, novels are essentially about the journey from innocence to experience, about discovering the reality underneath appearances.

Certain techniques, formulas—craft—increase the writer's (especially the beginner's) odds of entertaining the reader. Others mar and damage a story, often ruining its chances for sale. Why use them?

D. PARENTHETICAL REMARKS, STRAYING FROM THE STORY

If you're telling a friend a story you don't say, "and then, just when I turned the corner the guy who mugged me disappeared—oh, by the way, at the corner was this fantastic eerie light thrown off by this street lamp—" You don't tell your friend about the light from the street lamp because you know it's tangential to your story.

E. OVERWRITING

Overwriting is the equivalent of a comedian's "laying it in their laps." That is to say: saying what should remain unsaid. For example: Writing "John exclaimed" after an exclamation point is redundant—overwriting. Another example is, "Her large, ample bosom" when either "large" or "ample" will do. Overwriting does more than annoy the reader. Because of the lack of brevity, it insults his intelligence.

> "I try to leave out the parts that people skip."
>
> — Elmore Leonard

F. TELLING INSTEAD OF SHOWING

This is the most common failure of new writers. Readers don't want to merely be told a story through exposition and narrative. They want to have the story unfold. They want to figure things out for themselves, through the speech and behavior of the characters in scenes of action and dialogue. Even ancient storytellers must have known enough to avoid saying things like: "Little Wolf was very scared," or they'd find themselves alone in front of the campfire. Instead, they probably said something like, "Little Wolf could not get enough air. His mouth was dry and his hands dripped. He hoped the bear could not hear the thunder of his heart."

Telling

Janice was kind as she told him their romance was over. This made Joe's loss extra painful.

Showing

Janice's face was a ghostly heart shape, her eyes glowing with sympathy. She patted his shoulder gently.

"I really am so sorry." Her voice trembled. She picked a daisy from the grass and began to touch it. Then she wiped a tear from the corner of her eye. "It's not about you, Joe. And I'll always love you."

Joe wanted to yell at her, tell her how rotten she was. When she put her hand on his cheek, though, he felt his rage leave him. She withdrew her hand, sighing.

"We'll be friends," she said softly, "in spite of it all. I promise."

She kissed him once, and then vanished, leaving him with his unanswered pain and rage.

Telling

Charlie Harris was a little stinker. He messed up the kitchen floor, and his mother was driven to tears.

Showing

"Now, Charles," said his mother, Sally, "at least eat some of that delicious soup. You'll love it—it's full of vitamins. Yummy!"

"It's garbage!" Charlie yelled. As his mother turned away, he grinned, pleased because he was sure she was near tears.

As she wiped her eyes with a tissue, Charlie made his move. In one fast motion, he shoved the soup bowl off the table. It seemed to fly, landing on its side against the wall, then shattered into a thousand shards, spilling chicken and carrots and peas and greasy stock all over the freshly waxed floor.

Hurrying to pick up the mess, Sally slipped on a chunk of chicken and flopped onto the floor, her mouth agape.

"Charlie, I hate this!" she said, and began to sob.

Charlie shrugged. She always did that.

Telling

Jim was impressed with a beautiful woman when he first saw her.

Showing

Jim watched her approach, enjoying her firm, sensual body as she moved. When she noticed him, she became self-conscious.

When he saw her more clearly, he found pale gray eyes and a mass of wild black hair. Her nose was rather perky, with an endearing upturn. When she smiled, he felt a bit dizzy, and had to turn from her, pretending he saw something in the distance.

G. COINCIDENCE AND *DEUS EX MACHINA*

Certainly coincidence plays a part in real life, but has little value in fiction. What happens to a character should occur to a great extent as a result of his personality. However, coincidence which works *against* the character is fine to use, because it won't be construed by the reader as contrivance.

Deus Ex Machina

Webster explains it as follows:

> "A god from a machine (trans. from Greek). 1: a god introduced by means of a crane in ancient Greek and Roman drama to decide the final outcome. 2: a person or thing [as in fiction or drama] that appears or is introduced suddenly and unexpectedly and provides a contrived solution to an apparently insoluble difficulty."

Example: Moses and his people, chased by Egyptian soldiers, reach the Red Sea. He raises his staff and the sea parts. (It happens a second time when he raises his staff and the sea closes.) This doesn't happen in real life.

H. LACK OF SUBPLOTS

In most one hour TV dramas there are two or three stories running simultaneously. Ditto for novels. They can be related or unrelated. The related ones are best, as they can impinge on the outcome of the story.

Example: Four white cops in two police cars are doing routine patrol work. We get inside each man's head. The first is fuming, and he's sure his wife is playing around. The second is steamed up because his son was just kicked off the football team for taking drugs. The third has a medical problem, and a concerned doctor has taken a biopsy with the results coming in tomorrow. The fourth is a rookie who says, "If anything happens tonight I'm going to do exactly what my partner does."

A person who is DWI is driving a car at over 100 miles per hour. Two patrol cars stop the vehicle and a black man emerges. Suddenly the three begin to vent their frustrations on him with their billy clubs, and the rookie follows suit.

The plot is cops doing their "duty" by stopping a drunken driver. The beating is part of the plot. The subplots are how the personal lives of the men affect their behavior on duty. The final subplot is someone is filming it on a video camera.

I. LACK OF GOOD FORESHADOWING

What you *cannot* do is: A bridesmaid at a wedding is throwing confetti at the bride and groom. Suddenly, she is snatched by kidnappers and taken to a mountain cabin. Locked in a room she tries desperately to open the door and can't. Spotting a trap door, she finds it leads to a root cellar and then another exit. She leaves and follows the confetti she had previously left as a trail. When this is said *afterwards* it sounds contrived.

Suppose the bridesmaid, clutching a plastic bag of confetti, drops some along the way to leave a trail for the cops. *Then* when she leaves, she follows her own trail. The foreshadowing makes it plausible, particularly because it was thought through and she was given confetti by the author for the purpose in the first place. (More foreshadowing.)

When you go over your work before submitting it, be aware of the flaws mentioned in this chapter. If you find examples, exorcise them.

6

SOME MAJOR
MISTAKES IN STYLE

Readers don't want merely to be told a story. They want it shown, or dramatized or revealed—they want to figure out what's happening by themselves. To participate with the writer. These are some of the great pleasures of reading. These pleasures are intensified when the writer uses scenes of action and dialogue. They're diffused when the writer employs explanation, narration or introspection.

Beginners, especially, should use exposition, narration and characters' rumination to the barest minimum and scene, action and dialogue to the maximum.

When the writer has only one character on stage for too long there is a danger of too much introspection. Also, there can be little conflict unless two characters are present.

Stream-of-consciousness technique is best left to geniuses like James Joyce. Readers are not nearly as interested in what characters are thinking as in what they're doing.

Consequently, action is nearly always preferable to angst. Readers have their own angst, from which they want to escape.

A. DIALOGUE

Every character must sound different, unique from the rest. In a bad story or novel all the characters sound the same. Few things are more jarring or trying to the reader than passages of dialogue in which there is no variety.

Here's an example of differentiating well between the speech of characters:

> Jane: "I really find your attitude disgusting. You're coarse and crude, and I wouldn't consider renting this apartment to you."
>
> Joe: "Miss Big Deal, huh? Think you're a hot item? Who needs this damn rat hole—I can find better, easy."

In an attempt to clarify for the reader, writers often use identifiers: "John gulped," "Mary hissed," "Tom breathed," "Lenore simpered," "Jason thundered," and so on. All these means of identification and descriptions are the writer talking. "Said" is preferred to any and all of them.

"Said" has the additional advantage of becoming

invisible to the reader after a while. A most welcome dividend!

However, even the use of "said" can be overdone. Here is an excerpt from bestselling crime writer Robert B. Parker's novel *Double Deuce,* followed by criticism by Loren D. Estleman from *The New York Times* Book Review:

> "You working on anything?" Hawk said.
>
> "I was thinking about breakfast," I said.
>
> "I might need some support," Hawk said.
>
> "You might?"
>
> "Yeah. Pay's lousy."
>
> "How much?" I said.
>
> "I'm getting nothing."
>
> "I'll take half," I said.
>
> "You ain't worth half," Hawk said.

> "In the brief scene during which this conversation takes place, the phrase 'I said' appears 17 times; 'Hawk said' appears 10 times. Such tags, employed too frequently—in scenes involving only two speakers, they can be jettisoned altogether—stick up like sharp rocks, snagging the flow and reminding the reader that he is reading. It is Mr. Parker's most annoying mannerism, held over from all the other books in the series."

One of the most common errors new writers commit with dialogue is having their characters continually calling each other by name, to let the reader know who's speaking. This immediately strikes a false note with the reader, because in life people rarely call others by name in conversation:

"Hi, Sam, you going to the party?"

"No, Jim, I'm not."

"Why, Sam? It'll be fun."

"Well, Jim, maybe I'll think about it."

The reader can remember who's speaking for three short exchanges at least. To identify who's speaking repeatedly makes the reader feel he's being condescended to. Also, it's preferable to have a character say something followed by action, as in: "John pounded the desk for emphasis" rather than adding "John said."

Another common mistake among new writers is not separating narrative from dialogue with a new paragraph. Or, worse yet, not separating one character's dialogue from another's, as in the following example:

"I wish you'd come to the picnic, hon. I told everybody you'd be there. I can't, Harry—I'm just too busy Saturday. The guys will really be disappointed, Sherry, and Pam's looking forward to seeing you, too."

B. PRESENT TENSE

Many short stories and novels are being written in the present tense. However, many editors resist these stories. Their argument is that readers are not accustomed to non-traditional use of tenses and will avoid such stories and novels. The point here is that no editors are averse to stories written in the past tense. Why gamble?

No one has argued more persuasively against the rise of present tense than Rita Mae Brown in *Starting From Scratch A Different Kind of Writer's Manual*:

> Unfortunately, a rash of novels in the last decade have been written in the present tense. It's a fad and it won't last. There are good reasons for writing in the past tense.
>
> The first is familiarity. Every story we've read since 'The Iliad' has been written in past tense. Don't argue with thousands of years of success.
>
> The second reason is that the reader needs and wants distance and protection from the story. This safety zone, provided by the past tense, allows the reader eventually to open up for the emotional impact of the story. You've got to vault your reader's defenses. The reader doesn't want to get hurt, yet you want that reader to identify with your characters and that means to feel their pain and their joy. I feel strongly about this. Anyone who buys your book has plenty of

problems in his or her life. You have no moral right to disturb them unless you also entertain them. Art is moral passion married to entertainment. Moral passion without entertainment is propaganda, and entertainment without moral passion is television. By using the past tense (except in your dialogue, of course) you enable your reader to come to you.

The third reason to use past tense is technical. Do you want the reader to focus on the story or focus on your participles and gerunds? Don't distract a reader with your style. That's you showing off. A great style is one that appears effortless and one that is individual. Your voice should not sound like Faulkner's.

The fourth reason to use the past tense and not the present tense is: Why would anyone want to read a novel that sounds like a screenplay? Screenplays are in the present tense. They have to be. You're giving the director his marching orders. Fiction is not a screenplay. A screenplay can be a work of towering imagination but it will never be a novel. The two functions are unrelated. . . . I'm not disparaging screenplays. I've written seven of them and hope to write many more. I'm saying don't mix your mediums. It's trendy and you'll get attention for a while and then boom, it'll be over.

C. BASS ACKWARDS WRITING

Syntax, the arrangement of words in a sentence, is a valuable tool. The two ways in which emphasis is shown are (1) to place a particular word or words at the beginning or (2) the end of a sentence. Our term for placing words in the wrong order in a sentence is "bass ackwards" writing.

Bass Ackwards

At the construction site, the rod man called back to the surveyors various height readings for them to double check.

Correct

The rod man at the construction site called various height readings to the surveyors, for them to double check.

D. AUTHOR INTRUSION

A hundred years ago it was considered intimate and charming for Dickens to say, "Dear and gentle reader." Today, such a phrase would have the same intrusive effect as turning the lights on in the middle of a movie.

The best writers know enough not to call attention to

themselves by proselytizing or editorializing. Readers don't want a writer's opinion, they want to be entertained.

E. POINT OF VIEW

Jarring switches of point of view are a particular province of beginners. Generally one shouldn't give us a character's point of view unless we have been properly introduced to that character from the outset of a chapter or beginning of a story or after a break in a story.

Also, these words from John Ciardi about point of view in a single scene are most important: (The italics are ours.)

> *Within a single scene,* for example, it seems to be *unwise* to have access to the inner reflections of more than one character. *The reader generally needs a single character as the means of perception,* as the character to whom the events are happening, as the character with whom he is to empathize in order to have the events of the writing happen to him.

F. FRAME STORIES

The classic movie *Sunset Boulevard* is an example of a frame story. The movie opens with a man floating dead in a swimming pool. The rest of the film is one big flashback explaining how he got there. At the very end the viewer is back to the floating body. Frame stories are out of fashion.

G. FLASHBACKS

Flashbacks are allowed, but only if they're short and used under certain conditions. The biggest reason editors don't like flashbacks is that they stop the story. The reader hopefully has become hooked on the present events in the story and wants to find out how things are resolved. The flashback interrupts him.

Never use flashbacks at the beginning of a story and not until the reader is sufficiently hooked. Then use as brief a flashback as possible.

H. DREAMS

Dream sequences have long been out of favor with editors. To try to fool a reader into believing a dream is actually happening in the character's life is considered a cheap trick.

I. MIRROR, MIRROR

Describing a character who's looking into a mirror is another technique frowned on by editors. This technique has also been used too often. They much prefer you show the character through another character's eyes.

J. AUTHOR, AUTHOR

Fiction about a writer is a sign to the editor of another amateur writing autobiographically. Don't attempt this kind of story till you're well known.

K. NO SECRETS

Fooling the reader by withholding information is a cardinal sin for any writer but especially the mystery writer.

L. TIRED TALES

Overused plots, such as the mystery of how a character escaped a totally locked room, are a way to get your manuscript rejected quickly.

M. LACK OF ORGANIZATION

A novel takes a long time to write. Two months into the book, you'll have forgotten the color of the heroine's hair. Write out sketches of your main characters, then make a card index to include name, height, weight, age, hometown, schools attended, where he or she worked, relationships, married (yes/no) etcetera. When a character crops up in the story look at your index card.

One writer we know (a doctor) was confused about how to keep track of her anecdotes and stories. It bothered her. We suggested she use a couple of dozen folders and keep each story separate, then all she had to do was put each one in the correct folder.

7

How To Read
Like A Writer

*As a writer, I hold uncut pages to be comment
on an owner and an insult to an author. A book
for me is something to read, not kept under glass
or in a safe. I want to dogear it, to underline it,
to annotate it, and mark my favorite passages,
and make my own index on the blank pages at
the back.*

— John Mason Brown

Writers must learn to analyze by what techniques other
writers achieve their effects. Then they must emulate these
techniques, adding their own twists. If, for example, the
writer observes how J.D. Salinger characterized by showing what's in a character's medicine cabinet, then the writer

might characterize by showing what's in a character's desk or purse or locker.

Look at how Dick Francis in his brilliant novel *Straight* uses an office to characterize:

> I took in a few more details of the surroundings, beyond my first impression of gray. On the light greenish-gray of the carpet stood the armchair in charcoal and the desk in matte black unpainted and unpolished wood. The walls, palest gray, were hung with a series of framed geological maps, the frames black and narrow and uniform in size. The propped-open door, and another similar door to one side, still closed, were painted the same color as the walls. The total effect, lit by recessed spotlights in the ceiling, looked both straightforward and immensely sophisticated, a true representation of my brother.

If a writer studied the dialogue of Elmore Leonard he'd learn, for example, that Leonard eliminates as many words as possible at the beginning of a question so the sentence will be more artful because of brevity.

"Hell are you doing?" is much more powerful than, "What the hell are you doing?"

By studying the action scenes of Graham Greene, we learn, as Greene said, "to use only Anglo Saxon words in scenes of action."

In *Starting From Scratch A Different Kind of Writer's*

Manual, Rita Mae Brown says:

> Think, too, about deep emotion. You've fallen
> through the ice. You scream, "Help!" You do not
> yell, "Aid!" In times of greatest danger or heart-
> break even the most aristocratic of people will
> revert to Anglo-Saxon. As a writer, remember
> this, because it is the language of greatest emotive
> power.

In reading Hemingway's action scenes we learn that by
eliminating paragraphs, periods and commas the eye
speeds along with the action.

There is no greater teacher for the writer than reading
other writers. Period.

A fine way to judge writing is to take your favorite fiction and type up the first ten pages. Then read the manuscript pages and learn.

8

WHAT SLOWS THE READER?
WHAT SPEEDS HIM UP?

Semicolons slow the reader. Usually they can simply be deleted without notice. If not, substitute colons, which send the eye forward. Break up long sentences into two. As a last resort, use the comma which also slows the reader but not as much.

Dashes send the eye forward and speed the reader. But the love of dashes, common among new writers, takes away their power.

Looking at an entire page of long, run-on narrative without the breather of paragraphs intimidates and discourages most modern readers. Accessible stories and novels contain more paragraphs than inaccessible ones.

Chapters, too, have grown shorter over the years. With

all the competition from TV and movies, writers need to write shorter chapters. It's common nowadays for a chapter to be five or six pages. Certainly chapter length should be determined by what needs to be accomplished in a given chapter. And chapters can be a single page or two dozen if need be. However, in general—with a few exceptions—writers would be better off to not have their chapters exceed ten pages.

9

Characters Are
Not People

Readers expect and demand from protagonists (heroes and heroines) a higher set of morals and mores than they do real people. This is not to say that brave characters should suffer no fear. But they must overcome their fear, not allowing it to rule their lives.

A hero or heroine should always have a flaw or weakness that will cause the reader to think, perhaps unconsciously, "Why, he's human, after all!"

Do not characterize by saying, "He looked like Robert Redford." This is lazy writing, and is one of the cardinal sins that cause editors to throw manuscripts into the OUT mail box.

Telling the reader that a character is six foot or blue-eyed or blonde-haired does little to help him or her visualize them. It's also boring. But if he's "tall but stoop-shouldered," and his blue eyes "hold a constant look of hurt surprise" we know he has a hard time supporting his problems.

Descriptive characterization is best shown through the eyes, mouth, posture and gait.

Telling the reader a character is hard or mean or jovial is not what the reader wants. The reader doesn't want to be told but to observe and judge for himself. He wants the character to be revealed.

Only when a character is individualized—as good and likeable or fascinatingly evil—does the reader care what happens to him.

You may have a fine story whose plot turns as if on oiled ball bearings. But until the reader is moved emotionally he won't care, not even after the protagonist's frayed rope finally snaps, sending him falling thousands of feet to the rocks below.

On the other hand, if your character, a young woman shown as honest and kind, is being shot at by a despicable villain, the reader will fear for your young woman and hate your villain.

The following is an example of how Louis L'Amour makes us care about a character named Duncan in *The Quick And The Dead*.

Vallian noticed them, and shrugged. 'Riding back from Californy I counted more'n a thousand graves of folks that died or were killed last year.'

His amusement was ironic. 'I reckon some of them tried to go through to the gold fields with their wagons loaded too heavy.'

'Possibly,' Duncan said quietly, 'possibly they did just that. And perhaps some of them managed to get through, even though they were overloaded.'

'Mr. Vallian, were you ever married?'

'Me? Never.'

'Women, Mr. Vallian, often build their lives around things. The proper things in their proper places give women assurance, a sense of rightness and stability. Perhaps we men lack that, for better or worse, or maybe we have other things to which we give our attention.

'In this wagon we have a bed that my wife's family brought over from Devonshire almost two hundred years ago. We have several other articles of furniture equally as important. We could very easily have left these articles at home and loaded the space with food or implements, but the happiness of Susanna is important to me, and wherever we are, those things will be home to her. Do you understand, Mr. Vallian?'

In his extraordinary novel *Straight* Dick Francis makes us sympathetic to the narrator who, never having had a close relationship with his older brother, grieves for him when he's dying:

The tie of common blood was all that truly linked

Greville and me, and once it was undone there would be nothing left of him but memory. With regret I watched the pulse that flickered in his throat. When it was gone I would go back to my own life and think of him warmly sometimes, and remember this night with overall sorrow, but no more.

I went along to the waiting room for a while to rest my legs. The desperate young parents were still there, hollow-eyed and entwined, but presently a somber nurse came to fetch them, and in the distance, shortly after, I heard the rising wail of the mother's agonized loss. I felt my own tears prickle for her, a stranger. A dead baby, a dying brother, a universal uniting misery. I grieved for Greville most intensely then because of the death of the child, and realized I had been wrong about the sorrow level. I would miss him very much.

Incidentally, many writers start with a seemingly overwhelming villain. In this way, because the hero must measure up, great anticipation arises in the reader.

Here's an example from Louis L'Amour's *The Quick And The Dead*:

The Huron!
He was out here . . . he had to be. He had heard stories about the man. He was a skillful hunter, a

stalker of game, and he had killed more than one man. He was like a ghost in the woods, and in this timber along the river, he was in his element. Vallian strained his ears for sound, heard nothing. He straightened up, keeping himself merged with the brush, much of which was clumps of willow and some persimmon, and moved away. He was good, he told himself, but was he as good as the Huron? Was he even half as good?

Remember that every great hero deserves a great villain. Sherlock Holmes had Professor Moriarty. They were not evenly matched. Moriarty was shrewder, more resourceful.

Be careful when selecting opponents, i.e., protagonist and antagonist.

The following example explains it all.

Schwarzenegger is the hero (6'4"tall) against the villain Robert Redford (5'7" tall). If they got into a fight the reader and/or viewer would immediately sympathize with underdog Redford. So try to get the hero and villain evenly matched, or better yet, have the hero shorter and lighter. Then he breaks his hand before the big fight. Now you have a vulnerable yet sympathetic hero.

It's true that so-called "literary" novels sometimes have anti-heroes as protagonists, and often end on a "realistic" or "lifelike" down note.

However, the great majority of readers read to get the satisfaction which real life seldom offers. They seek the illusion that there is order in the world—hard work will be rewarded and good will triumph over evil. The reader wants to be lifted, at least temporarily, out of the dullness and unpredictability of his own life into a world of excitement with an eventual harmonious ending.

According to Mario Vargas Liosa in *A Writers Reality*, fiction doesn't exist so much to provide an escape from the world but to give readers better maps with which to navigate through it.

> One of the major contributions of literature in our lives is that it establishes an artificial order of the world, of time, of space, of the living experience. . . . When you explore the possibilities of creating a time structure in a story, you are not only doing something that is an artificial achievement and the achievement of a formal skill. . . . You are also creating an instrument through which we can better understand how daily experience, living experience, is happening in reality. And so this fascination with time, which is a distinct characteristic of modern literature, is not gratuitous, not artificial. It is a way of reacting to a reality in which we feel ourselves—particularly in contemporary society—totally lost. We are becoming so insignificant, so minor in this extraordinary and impersonal world, which is the world of modern societies, that we need a way to place ourselves in it. This artificial organization that literature gives to life is something that helps us in real life to feel less lost and confused.

In order to give the reader what he's looking for most—
a logical link of cause and effect and a satisfying conclusion—you must have characters who react uncharacteristically
to situations.

A character may be drawn several ways. You can simply
tell the reader through exposition: "John was kind to people he needed to impress for business purposes but cruel
to his wife and children." Or, he may be drawn by describing the character, which is also expository: "His move-
ments were slow and seemingly without purpose, but he
always managed to get where he wanted to go on time."

Or, by giving the character's thoughts: "One more mar-
tini," John thought, "and she'll be play-clay."

The above are examples of static writing. During exposition or introspection the story doesn't move forward. By
far the best way to characterize is through action. If you
show a man walking through an airline terminal checking
every phone booth for forgotten change, the reader has the
pleasure of deciding for himself some of what the character
is all about.

Dialogue, too, moves the story ahead while giving the
reader the joy of figuring out the character for himself.

The character who says to the taxi driver, "Do you travel outside of Manhattan?" is much different from the character who says, "Look, buster, I know the law says you have
to take me to Brooklyn and I've got your license number
and name, so don't give me any lip."

Names are more important than most beginning writers
know. Willy Jones, for instance, would be suitable for a simple, small town boy. The name Lyman Van Horn, on the

other hand, indicates a sophisticate from a powerful family living in the city. There are many books which give the meanings and origins of names which are most helpful in choosing what to call your characters.

The most unforgettable characters are complex, quirky. The best way to accomplish this is to give your players conflicting character traits.

The hooker with a heart of gold and the mobster who adores his mother have become clichés. But because every one of us has many sets of conflicting traits the possibilities are endless. Consider the jittery gemcutter, the judge who can't make a personal decision, the clergyman with a large libido.

It's most important to remember that you can't just characterize once. You must continue to characterize as your story moves forward.

10

"But It Happened In Real Life!"

Fiction is not intended to be a mirror of real life. Rather, it is the distillation, the essence, the flavor of it. Real life is most often too chaotic to have the interpretative shape and form fiction demands.

Readers usually have had all they can take of the chaos in their own lives when they turn to the comforting order of fiction. They need to believe that the errant knight will rescue the damsel in distress or the murder will be solved or that love will be requited.

If you deprive the reader of his illusion, no amount of "But it happened in real life!" will comfort him. He knows all too well about the hazards of real life. That's exactly why he tried to escape into fiction.

There lies the danger of autobiographical fiction—which, unfortunately, is what most beginning fictioneers write.

It invariably takes a highly crafted professional to be able to avoid the booby-traps of autobiographical fiction. A professional who can see even his own parents and siblings with cool, clear unemotional sight. A professional who can separate what was poignant and fascinating to him once from what will have the same effect on a reader now.

So, if you're a beginner, avoid autobiographical fiction. Your journal entries or history of the family will be fascinating to the family, but don't think that anything close to them—without added invention and drama, without scenes and characters—will interest editors.

11

BEGINNINGS

Titles are the very first thing an editor or reader sees of your work. They must grab attention, seduce, ask the question: What can the writer mean?

J.D. Salinger's story, "A Perfect Day For Bananafish" has such a title. So does Truman Capote's novel, *Breakfast at Tiffany's*.

Oxymorons often make fine titles such as this one from a former *Writer's Digest* student: "The Nineteen Year Old Geriatric." Another is *Urban Cowboy*.

OPENING SENTENCES AND PARAGRAPHS

First sentences must continue to seduce and draw the reader in. "Tomorrow they would break both her legs," is the opening of a story about a woman facing corrective surgery in the morning. "The head of the missing person's bureau was missing" is the opener from a classic mystery. "Kate Dunn wondered how long it would be before anyone discovered that she'd murdered Eva" is the opening line of a story by another ex-student of ours.

The opener of *The Catcher in the Rye* does exactly what a beginning sentence should do.

"If you really want to hear about it, the first thing you'll probably want to know is where I was born, and what my lousy childhood was like, and how my parents were occupied and all before they had me, and all that David Copperfield kind of crap, but I don't feel like going into it, if you want to know the truth."

A reviewer said of Dick Francis's beginning of *Straight*: "If you read the first paragraph of *Straight*, I'm willing to wager, whatever the odds, you will sprint to the finish line."

Judge for yourself: "I inherited my brother's life. Inherited his desk, his business, his gadgets, his enemies, his horses and his mistress. I inherited my brother's life, and it nearly killed me."

Here's another brilliant beginning paragraph from Eric Ambler's *The Case of Time*: "The warning message arrived on Monday, the bomb itself on Wednesday. It became a busy week."

There was a time not too long ago in which leisurely openings were fashionable. Steinbeck, for one, began many a story or novel with a description of the setting. But alas, for such times—and such words as alas.

Many aspiring writers of fiction begin a story from the beginning, no doubt taking their cue from sagas like *Tom Jones*, which commence even before the birth of the hero or heroine.

As a rule it's best to begin a story or novel at a turning point in the main character's life.

Listen to Frank Chambers' famous opening sentence in James M. Cain's *The Postman Always Rings Twice*: "They threw me off the hay truck about noon."

Already we know quite a lot about where Chambers has been, and we sense that he's about to get into trouble again.

Not very much later Cain gives us a superb turning point in Chambers' life: "Hell could have opened for me then, and it wouldn't have made any difference. I had to have her, if I hung for it."

12

WHY A NOVELIST SHOULD FIND HIS NICHE

Because of the awesome ongoing explosion of information, more and more professionals of every kind have become specialists. In medicine, general practitioners are a dying breed. In their places are internists who specialize.

Tax attorneys don't get involved in accident cases. Accountants limit themselves to individuals or corporations.

It's the same with publishing. Visit even the most humble independent bookshop and you'll find books divided into fiction and nonfiction, mystery, romance, adventure, sci-fi, spy, horror, western, etcetera. And the list continues to grow. Tom Clancy created a whole new genre called the "techno thriller." Suspense is a sub genre of mystery. Then there's romantic suspense and . . . you get the idea.

A book salesperson has only a few moments to present

the busy bookstore owner or manager with a pitch on each book on his publishers' list. If he can't categorize a novel the salesperson has a much harder job.

With the high cost of books, buyers demand to have their choices pigeon-holed as much as possible.

For these reasons authors are sold as "mystery writers" or "masters of the macabre."

The advantages to the writer are many. Firstly, his books sell better when the public is able to tell what kind of novel to expect from him. Secondly, because the specializing writer must become an expert in what has and is being written in his chosen genre, he avoids writing what's old hat.

Far too few aspiring novelists are aware of the advantages of specialization. Even fewer understand that it is their contemporaries they should be reading and not past masters, who used styles and techniques many of which are unsuitable for today's market. Examples are author's intrusion and predominance of narrative.

13

Length

If you were a carpenter commissioned to build a dining room table and you built that table so high that your patrons had to reach up to eat their food, you would have failed.

Regardless of how well you had selected your wood with the most symmetrical configuration of grains, or how splendidly you carved your designs or sanded or stained you would not have done your job because the table wouldn't be usable.

The same is true of trying to sell a short story say of 10,000 words. Who will buy it? Certainly no slick magazine where the average short story is approximately seven double-spaced typewritten pages of 250 words (25 lines with 10 words a piece) equalling about 1,750 words. No commercial magazine is going to restructure its format even if you can write like Tolstoy.

Writers have the best chance of getting published with a short short story of say 500 words because 1) this is a length that makes an editor's pagination job (selecting and arranging of material on the page) easier and 2) most writers can't successfully pull off a story in so little space.

It's most important that aspiring short story writers read contemporary stories in magazines. The length of the average story has shortened over the decades. In Scott Fitzgerald's time it was not unusual to see stories of 10,000 words. Today this would constitute a novelette, a form for which, like its longer cousin, the novella, there is almost no market at all.

Too many amateurs have a fantasy that an editor will see the seeds of genius in their work and will, as Maxwell Perkins did, especially with Thomas Wolfe, help them to cut, prune and polish their work into immortality.

Unfortunately, today's crop of editors simply do not have the time or the freedom to do this kind of editing. Commercial magazines and publishers are, in most cases, now owned by huge conglomerates who measure success by net profits.

Their philosophy is that they'd rather pay more to the established professional than take the time to groom the amateur.

Therefore, to a great extent, the newcomer's fiction has to be even better than the professional's.

All of these are sad facts. But they are facts, nonetheless, and nostalgia for the "good old days" won't bring the aspiring short story writer or novelist a millimeter closer to publication.

One must accept these facts and attempt to overcome them. How? By learning to write better than his competitors. By studying the markets and submitting exactly the kind of fiction a particular publisher is looking for in exactly perfect form.

In our work as readers/editors working through the recommendations of literary agents and publishers, we have not found it surprising that the best writers are also those people who know that a mystery novel is about 60,000 words while a family saga is usually 100,000 or better. Invariably the best written stories and novels are submitted on heavy weight bond printed out in letter quality.

14

EGGPLANT PROSE

"Read over your compositions and, when you meet a passage which you think is particularly fine, strike it out."

— Samuel Johnson

The best writing is that which doesn't call attention to itself. Such writing is usually so simple and direct that non-writers believe it has been easy to do. Professionals know that's anything but true.

Simple writing means few or no metaphors, similes and alliterations. It means using nouns and verbs instead of adjectives and adverbs.

Finally, forward motion in any piece of writing is carried by verbs. Verbs are the action words of the language and the most important. Turn to any passage on any page of a successful novel and notice the high percentage of verbs. Beginning writers always use too many adjectives and adverbs and generally use too many dependent clauses. Count your words and words of verbal force (like that word 'force' I just used)."

— William Sloan in *The Craft of Writing*

Simple writing means being active and not passive, like saying, "She's talented" instead of "She's not without talent."

Here's an editorial letter from William Sloan to novelist Ernest K. Gann:

"Avoid words like 'almost,' try to avoid the passive voice in your verbs . . . 'His blue eyes commanded their interest . . . seemed fixed upon some distant object . . . pursuing someone . . . many felt obliged . . . experienced a sense of disappointment' is all bad writing, sawdust stuff. Damn it, Gann, when you get off the beam you get rhetorical as hell . . ."

If you find yourself holding on tenaciously to poetic or purple (eggplant) prose, a red flag should arise in your mind.

"Whenever you feel an impulse to perpetuate a piece of exceptionally fine writing, obey it . . . and delete it before sending your manuscript to the press."

— Sir Arthur Quiller-Couch

There's an anecdote about the great sculptor Rodin that may help make our point. One day while he was giving a new apprentice a tour of his studio, the student suddenly stopped in front of a statue of a man and woman embracing.

"My God, master, these feet of the woman—of both of them—are magnificent!"

With that Rodin grabbed a mallet from a nearby table and with one sure swift blow struck off the two sets of entangled feet.

"But why master?" the shocked apprentice implored.

"Because in art no part is ever more important than the whole."

As an example of purple prose here's the winning entry for the 10th annual Bulwer-Lytton Fiction Contest for wretched writing. The contest, sponsored by San Jose State University, was named for Victorian novelist Edward Bulwer-Lytton, who unwittingly inspired writers and cartoon characters alike with his opening line, "It was a dark and stormy night."

"As the newest Lady Turnpot descended into the kitchen wrapped only in her celery-green dressing gown, her creamy bosom rising and falling like a temperamental soufflé, her tart mouth pursed in distaste, the sous-chef whispered to the scullery boy, 'I don't know what to make of her . . .'"

Some other winners included:

Children's literature: "Santa, bruised and bloodied from his encounter with a mountain peak, surveyed the damage: his sled a write-off, the presents hopelessly scattered, and 50 days hike to the North Pole, but at least he had lots of venison."

Vile puns: "'You can run,' shouted Scotland Yard's Inspector Boothroyd in triumph as he clutched the last remaining bottle of noxious potion and watched Dr. Jekyll leap to freedom through the shattered laboratory window, 'but you can't Hyde.'"

In his classic, *The Art of Writing* Sir Arthur Quiller-Couch said:

"All reading demands an effort. The energy, the good-will which a reader brings to the book is, and must be, partly expended in the labor of reading, marketing, learning, inwardly digesting what the author means. The more difficulties, then, we authors obtrude on him by obscure or careless writing, the more we blunt the edge of his attention: so that if only in our own interest—though I had rather keep it on the ground of courtesy—we should study to anticipate his comfort."

15

FIRST DRAFTS

A common problem with aspiring writers is that they have the notion that the better the first draft the better the finished story or novel to come. They feel that they must labor over each word and sentence to achieve perfection.

Nothing could be more false.

We tell our clients that during a first draft nothing should impede the progress. If the writer can't think of a name for a character, it's best to just call him "he" or "the policeman" or simply leave a blank space.

Here is what some have said about first drafts.

> "I write any sort of rubbish which will cover the main outlines of the story, then I begin to see it."
>
> — Frank O'Connor

"The first draft of anything is shit."

— Ernest Hemingway

"Just get it down on paper, and then we'll see what to do with it."

— Maxwell Perkins' advice
to Marcia Davenport

Beginning writers often believe that writing fiction is easy for professionals and because it's different for them they may lack the gifts to be a short story writer or a novelist.

"I'm a bleeder. It's a good day when I get a page done."

— S.J. Pereleman

16

DOES IT END OR MERELY STOP?

"Great is the art of beginning, but greater is the art of ending."

— Longfellow

"Between beginning and end, everything in the novel (story) happens, everything must happen. What happens could be called the process of the novel (story). By way of contrast, a dictionary also has a process but it is wholly an alphabetical process, from aardvark to zoril. When a dictionary runs out of letters it stops. There is something of an analogy here because when a novel (story) completes its process it, too, stops."

—William Sloan in *The Craft of Fiction*

This is not to say that every single loose end need be tied up in fiction. And certainly fine fiction asks more questions than it answers or can answer.

But stories and novels must end with a resolution to the problem or conflict or the overcoming of the obstacle.

Downbeat endings are popular in so-called "literary" fiction which aims to show that characters, like people, usually lose in life.

Readers don't read to get discouraged or depressed. Satisfy your readers with an upbeat ending. This does not mean an off-into-the-sunset finale but one that offers hope to the reader.

Endings create problems for many writers, who are often a bit tired and less confident as they come to the end of a story. There is so much to be accomplished in an ending, and if the ending fails, the story fails. It's vital to know the basic elements of a good ending.

A. RESOLUTION

An ending must give the reader the impression that every word has been written that was needed—nothing else has to be done. All is *resolved*. This doesn't mean that the ending has to be a clichéd happy one. While most editors, especially commercial ones, prefer endings which promise good developments and a change in the main character, they prefer the endings to be subtle.

B. SURPRISE

If you can write some kind of surprise into your ending, it is like giving the reader a bonus. Be sure the surprise is credible. If you haven't planned the surprise, be sure to go back and validate it. Insert a few lines early in the story to make the surprise seem reasonable later on. You must be careful not to telegraph the surprise by giving too much away.

C. TONE AND MOOD

If your story has been written in a light tone, keeping a pleasant mood, it is wrong to change it at the end, and vice versa. Readers choose stories partly because of the tone, selecting those which fit their own moods, and any sharp departure in tone is very jarring, a kind of breach of contract.

D. UNFINISHED BUSINESS

It's vital to be sure you haven't left plot lines unfinished, details not haven't followed through on. If you announce on page three that Aunt Matilda's will is going to be read, and then don't let the reader know how that turns out, you will have an angry, unsettled reader. When doing your final drafts you must check to be sure you haven't left any such matters unattended. If you have, be sure you need the material. Perhaps your instincts were good—the material wasn't important—and that's why you didn't finish the plot line. If so, just cut every trace out. If not, you have more writing to do.

E. NOTHING NEW, PLEASE

When a bit tired and discouraged, many writers are tempted to add a new character at the end of a story, or to create new plot lines or settings or crises. This can be fatal. The reader doesn't want to deal with anything new—he or she is concentrating on what has gone before, and wants to see it all brought to an *organic, satisfying resolution.*

17

CHANGE: A BASIC
TENET OF ALL FICTION

It's true that the main character doesn't have to change at the end of a story in order for the story to be successful. But it certainly helps. We urge every newcomer to take full advantage of the reader satisfaction that a positive change in a main character gives to a story.

Let's go back for a moment to a statement in the earlier section called, INCIDENT VERSUS STORY: *A story is an unfolding of events coming from a problem and resulting in the resolution of that problem.*

Now let's add to that statement this: *and a change in the main character.*

At the end the main character must see himself and the world differently than he saw it at the beginning.

Let's say this in other words: A story begins with a character who has a problem. The problem gets worse. Just when the reader believes the character will lose out the character figures out how to resolve the problem. As a result of the struggle with his problem the character learns to see himself differently and he changes.

18

REVISION AND REWRITING

"The best writing is rewriting."

— E.B. White

"The difference between the right word and the nearly right word is the same as that between lightning and the lightning bug."

— Mark Twain

"The last thing that we find in making a book is to know what we must put first."

— Blaise Pascal

"I have written—often several times—every word

I have ever published. My pencils outlast their erasers."

— Vladimir Nabokov

"I write slowly because I write badly. I have to rewrite everything many, many times just to achieve mediocrity."

— William Gass

"Most writers slough off the toughest but most important part of their trade—editing their stuff, honing it and honing it until it gets an edge like a bullfighter's killing sword."

— Ernest Hemingway

"Revision is just as important as any other part of writing and must be done con amore.*"*

— Evelyn Waugh

"Nothing you write, if you hope to be any good will ever come out as you first hoped."

— Lillian Hellman

"I can't write five words but that I change seven."

— Dorothy Parker

In the finest book we've found on revision and rewriting: *Getting the Words Right: How to Review, Edit and Rewrite (Writer's Digest* Books) the author, Theodore Cheney, quotes from an extract of an interview Ernest Hemingway gave to George Plimpton of the *Paris Review*:

> *Paris Review*: How much rewriting do you do?
>
> Hemingway: It depends. I rewrote the ending to *A Farewell To Arms*, the last page of it, thirty-nine times before I was satisfied.
>
> *Paris Review*: Was there some technical problem there? What was it that had stumped you?
>
> Hemingway: Getting the words right.

Nothing separates the amateur from the professional so much as the amount of revising and rewriting he is willing to do on his manuscript.

Many an amateur suffers from the misconception that the closer the first draft is to the last draft the better a writer he is.

There is absolutely no correlation to the amount of drafts a writer requires to get the words right and that of a writer's ability.

However, a general rule is that the more drafts a writer labors through the better the finished product.

No less a writer than John Updike has spoken of how, at the beginning of his career he would test every single adjective and verb he used in a short story against possible better ones in his thesaurus.

Many writers have said that writing *is* rewriting. Painters have long known the value of refining their efforts. Here's the Random House dictionary definition of the painting term pentimento: "the presence or emergence of earlier images, forms or strokes that have been changed and painted over."

Before revising a story or novel one must read it through once, forsaking the nitty gritty for great reductions and removals. In fact anything—whole chapters even—should be deleted if they don't move the story forward. Afterward reduce or remove extraneous and ineffective sentences and words.

Next, any part of the manuscript that is tangential or not organic has to be rethought and rearranged. Parts have to be put into the proper proportion to the whole.

Finally there's the polishing work: choosing active verbs over adjectives and adverbs, selecting the best word, listening for just the right sound, rhythm and pacing.

Rewriting obviously begins with the whole and general, and ends with the parts and the specific. It is, after the white heat of composing, the area of writing where the most craft is employed.

A CHECKLIST OF FAULTS

1. Missed opportunities—are the big scenes onstage or off?

2. Is your protagonist a survivor or a victim?

3. Does your characters' speech reflect who they are or do they all talk alike?

4. Is your antagonist or villain a pushover?

5. Do you have too many substitutes for "said" or do you let the dialogue itself carry the load?

6. Do you have long stretches where the reader is not given the break of paragraphs?

7. Do you grab the reader's attention right from the title and the first sentence?

8. Have you segued in your research or is it obvious?

9. Does your main character see himself and the world differently at the end than he did at the beginning?

10. Is the weather consistent with the seasons?

11. Has your protagonist solved his problem or did someone else (or coincidence) intercede?

12. Is your protagonist interesting and someone we care about?

19

Common Law Copyright

By far the question most commonly asked by newcomers is: "How do I know they won't steal my idea?"

Firstly, there are no new ideas. It's the delivery that counts.

Secondly, the law gives you greater rights in your manuscript before it's formally copyrighted than you'll have afterward.

Unpublished works fall under the heading of "common-law copyright." This means that your work is internationally protected until the day of publication at which time the publisher will take out a statutory copyright in your name.

There's no need to go to the trouble and expense of copyrighting your work in Washington, D.C. If you're still concerned, mail yourself a certified copy of your manuscript (return receipt requested) and keep it sealed until the time it may be needed.

20

FINDING FACTS FAST

It's best to get your written information first. This way
when you eventually talk to experts in the field you'll be
knowledgeable enough to ask the right questions to get the
most out of your interviews.

A. LIBRARIES

There are three basic kinds of libraries: public, college and
special libraries. The best public libraries are usually main
branches, which are most likely to contain large reference
collections.

College libraries open to the public can be found by
contacting the Association of College and Research
Libraries, American Library Association, 50 Huron Street,

Chicago, IL 60611; 312-944-6780.

Special libraries specialize in a particular subject—drugs, baseball, Africa, astronomy, marketing and countless other subjects. Most specialty libraries are open to the public, some by appointment only.

One kind of special library is the corporate library. CBS's library, for example, contains a wealth of information about broadcasting, while Exxon's has extensive data about energy. Contact the Special Libraries Association, 1700 18th Street NW, Washington, D.C. 20069; 202-234-4700. Ask to speak to an "Information Specialist." These experts will help you identify a special library in the area you need.

Many libraries, like the New York Public Library, have phone information services. For no charge a researcher will try to answer, "When was the automobile invented?" or "What is the flying time from New York to Zurich?"

Two of the very best, if basic, sources of information in a library are the *New York Times* Index and the Magazine Index.

The *Times* is a newspaper of record. Usually the libraries will provide the newspaper on microfilm. Often the summary of the article included in the index itself will provide all the information you need.

The Magazine Index is an automated system which provides the user with a display of the index on a special microfilm terminal. About 400 general-interest programs are indexed. Approximately 3,000 libraries throughout the country have this index available.

Some other useful sources of information in the library are:

Readers' Guide to Periodic Literature
Business Periodicals Index
Subject Guide to Books in Print

B. OTHER SOURCES

To find out-of-print books try the Strand Bookstore at 828 Broadway, New York, New York 10003, 212-473-1452. The Strand stocks over two and a half million books.

Book search companies advertise in the book review section of *The New York Times, Washington Post* and other literary publications.

Other fine sources of information are magazine and newsletter directories such as:

Ulrich's International Periodicals Directory
IMS Directory of Publications
Standard Periodical Directory
Magazine Industry Market Place
Newsletter Yearbook Directory
Oxbridge Directory of Newsletters

Then there are the "people information" references:

Who's Who
Current Biography

Biography Index
Biography and Genealogy
New York Times Obituaries Index

The US Government is one of the very best sources of information.

National Technical Information Service
Library of Congress
Bureau of the Census
States First Abstract of the United States
Government Printing Office

C. SPECIALIZED BOOKSTORES

The yellow pages of the larger cities group bookstores into specific subject areas. In New York City's yellow pages, for example, you'll see bookstores specializing in Africa, art, mystery, fiction, astrology, architecture, science fiction, cooking, health, occult, travel, performing arts, women, etcetera.

D. DATABASES

BRS, Latham, New York
CompuServe, Columbus, Ohio

DelMar, Cambridge, Massachusetts
Dialing Information Services, Palo Alto, California
The Source, Arlington, Virginia
VV/TEXT, Philadelphia, Pennsylvania

In addition, some organizations, especially government agencies, make databases available for free. Check a copy of the *Federal Database Finder*, published by Information USA (Potomac, MD).

Check out a book called *Databasics* (Garland Publishing) for everything you need to know about finding information by computers. Here are three other sources.

Directory of Online Data Bases (Cuadra/Elsevier) lists over 3,000 online databases and is updated quarterly.

Computer Readable Databases (American Library Association)

Data Base Directory (Knowledge Industry Publishers)

E. EXPERTS

Now that you've got your written information down let's talk about what we consider the greatest resource an information-seeking fiction writer has: people.

We have never once had an expert we called on for research turn us down. In fact, most experts are delighted to help—especially if you promise them a thank you in your book.

There are many writers who pay information experts to do their research. While there is certainly nothing ethically wrong in this, we believe a lot of the thrill in discovering fascinating facts is lost this way. This has to result in dampening a writer's overall passion for a project. And a writer's passion must always come through in his writing.

Part II

SOME
IMPORTANT
QUESTIONS

21

WHEN IS IT PLAGIARISM?

"Immature artists imitate. Mature artists steal."

— Lionel Trilling

If one copies another's actual prose that is plagiarism. But in fiction one is free to use plots, stories, ideas and, most importantly, techniques as starting points.

For example, the story of *Frankenstein* is constantly being retold in a new form. Likewise the plot from *The Boy Who Cried Wolf* is always being updated. *Romeo and Juliet* is derived from *Tristan and Isolde* and Shakespeare bragged that the ideas for all of his works were "borrowed."

Technique may be the richest ground from which to glean good writing.

In *Moby Dick* Melville describes in great detail the

forging of a harpoon and then has Ahab devise such an elaborate christening for the weapon that when the harpooner finally throws it at the great whale we almost feel the lance viscerally hitting its target.

Melville gave credit for this technique to Homer's craft in depicting how Achilles' shield grew under Hephaestus' hammer. In both cases we're intrigued by the process of manufacture instead of being bored by a description of the ready-made article. Also we're cunningly flattered in a sense that the shield or, in Melville's case, the harpoon, is being made for *us*.

The point is stories, plots and techniques have almost always been taken from past writers. By all means help yourself.

22

WHAT ABOUT ATTITUDE?

A writer's attitude has a great deal to do with whether he gets published. A very talented writer with poor attitude will not get published. A writer with average talent but a great attitude will, often, we have found, get published in time.

POOR ATTITUDE

- Back in the golden days of publishing I would've been discovered by a Maxwell Perkins.

- There are only a handful of magazines who publish fiction now.

GREAT ATTITUDE

- There's no sense wasting time thinking about the so-called golden days.

- Counting the "little magazines" there are more opportu-

• It's not fair that most magazines and publishers won't read my manuscripts without an agent.

• Because society has gone to the dogs, people don't read as much fiction any more, further reducing my chances.

• I have great ideas, so a publisher should look beyond frivolous things like whether or not I'm entertaining or if I paid someone a fortune to do a perfect typing job.

nities for getting a story published than ever before.

• I'm going to do whatever I can to get an agent.

• Because less fiction is read nowadays, I have to learn to write even better and market even harder.

• The world will do just fine without my novel or short story. I need to polish my manuscript till an editor simply can't refuse to accept it and then present it perfectly.

23

WHAT ABOUT
WRITER'S BLOCK?

"Every writer I know has trouble writing."

— Joseph Heller

One of the basic misconceptions about writing that is constantly being perpetuated is writer's block.

We've all seen the cliché scene in the movies in which a writer is shown tearing a sheet of paper from his typewriter, crushing it into a ball and flinging it into a wastebasket as he reaches desperately for his muse for inspiration.

If writers only wrote in the presence of their muses, they'd starve. A professional writes when inspired, but also when he's not even in the mood.

"I quit writing if I feel inspired, because I know I'm going to have to throw it away. Writing a novel is like building a wall brick by brick; only amateurs believe in inspiration."

— Frank Yerby

"Inspiration comes out of the act of making an artifact, a work of craft."

— Anthony Burgess

"Like a lot of what happens in novels, inspiration is a sort of spontaneous combustion—the oily rags of the head and heart."

— Stanley Elkin

"When I sit at my table to write, I never know what it's going to be till I'm underway. I trust in inspiration, which sometimes comes and sometimes doesn't. But I don't sit back waiting for it. I work *every* day.

— Alberto Moravia

"Writing is easy; all you do is sit staring at a blank sheet of paper until the drops of blood form on your forehead."

— Gene Fowler

No one has written more intelligently about so-called "writer's block" than Peter Elbow in *Writing Without Teachers*. This is the best book we know about how to get unstuck in your writing.

The basic premise is that writers who get "blocked" are placing too much importance on their first draft. The book tries to free the writer to write by greatly lowering expectations attached to the first draft. And it works!

"I'm up against a stone wall, I'll never finish this story (book)."

There is the widespread illusion among beginners that if they don't know where they're going with their story or novel that their projects are doomed.

Unfortunately, only pros know from experience that often the writer does not and cannot know the way.

"We work in our own darkness a great deal with little real knowledge of what we are doing."

— John Steinbeck

This is especially true in the long work like a novel. Professionals have learned that writing is a process. And that not only can't a writer know in advance exactly where his novel will always take him, it wouldn't be ideal if he could. After all, if the writer is surprised certainly the reader will be more apt to be so.

"No tears in the writer, no tears in the reader, no surprises for the writer, no surprises for the reader."

— Robert Frost

Sometimes writers "talk out" what they should be writing—result: blank pages.

"I just think it's bad to talk about one's present work, for it spoils something at the root of the creative act. It discharges the tension."

— Norman Mailer

"I have a suspicion that if I talk about plot, it's like letting sand out of a hole in the bottom of a bag."

— Shirley Hazzard

"You lose it if you talk about it."

— Ernest Hemingway

One of the hardest things about a writing session is getting started. Here's some advice from novelist (*The Secret of Santa Vittoria*) Robert Crichton:

I developed one tactic about writing that other writers might be able to profit from. I call it across the river and into the prose. During the

Second World War a friend of mine serving in the Alaska Scouts noticed that when an American squad came to a river near the end of the day the squad would ford the river so they could build fires and dry their equipment and be dry when starting out in the morning. The squads with Indians always stopped on the near shore. The reason for this was another facet of immersion. In the morning the Americans, comfortable, warm and dry would tend to move very carefully and slowly across the tundra to avoid getting wet. They would detour for miles to avoid crossing a stream. The Indians on the other hand would start the day by fording the river and they didn't give a damn what happened to them after that. The worst had already been done.

I felt this could be applied to writing. There is a desire to finish a paragraph or chapter and enjoy the satisfaction of finishing. It is a good feeling. But in the morning there now is only that empty white blank sheet of paper to be filled. I have wasted days trying to regain a momentum I have lost. Now I don't allow myself the luxury of finishing, of getting dry and comfortable. When I am going good but have worked enough for the day I stop in the middle of a sentence. It is irritating and frustrating but also effective. There is nothing in writing harder to do than to start. But in the morning I finish the sentence that has been left unfinished and then I finish the paragraph and all at once I am in the river again.

E.L. Doctorow has said:

"Writing is like driving at night. You can see only as far as the headlights, but you can make the whole trip that way."

Amen.

Student: But this isn't the novel I wanted to write.

Teacher: Listen to these words from John Steinbeck:

"In utter loneliness a writer tries to explain the unexplainable. And sometimes if he is very fortunate and if the time is right, a very little of what he is trying to do trickles through . . ."

Student: Yes, but I planned on having more surrealism in there. You know, magic, like the South American novelists?

Teacher: Yes, I know. Look, someone wiser than me once said, "I write to see what I'm thinking."

Student: I don't like what I'm thinking.

Teacher: (Desperately) No one reaches up to his vision of a novel. Think what Tolstoy and Melville must have aspired to.

Student: I can't stop thinking about myself.

Exactly. This student writer is more concerned with what he has to say and how he says it than whether he's written entertaining fiction.

"We do not write as we want but as we can."

— W. Somerset Maugham

24

CAN YOU AFFORD
TO BE A WRITER?

"A writer can make a fortune in America but he can't make a living."

— James Michener

Truman Capote wrote a novel entitled *Answered Prayers* in which characters achieved their dreams and discovered that it wasn't what they wanted after all.

Many aspiring writers who succeed in getting published find out they can't afford to be writers.

There are many reasons why being broke at times is inevitable for most professional writers.

Even professionals have periods where they can't produce or what they've produced doesn't work.

On occasion, changes in the market leave a pro in the

position of a clothing manufacturer with a factory full of Nehru jackets. At other times, manuscripts sit on editors' desks for months as if in some literary limbo. There are times when publishers have a cash flow problem which is passed along to the writer. Sometimes a publisher decides his list is too long and decides not to publish a book which he's already paid for. The writer gets to keep his advance but can forget royalties, foreign sales and all other ancillary rights sales.

Of course being broke is not the same as being poor. Writing can be most rewarding in ways other than money. But the stress of not being able to earn a living does much to erode those rewards.

For that reason many professional writers have back-up ways of earning a living. Having experience as a waitress, bartender or short order cook is more valuable than say, knowledge of writing ad copy because the former are jobs one can get quickly and hold onto as long as necessary.

Opinions vary as to which types of jobs are best for writers. Some, like Steinbeck, believe that writers should only do manual work so as not to drain their creativity.

On the other hand, many of our best writers, like Hemingway and Crane, were able to write while working as journalists.

Each writer has to discover what's best for him or her.

25

WHO SHOULD
TELL YOUR STORY?

A. FIRST PERSON

First person has certain innate bonuses: directness, immediacy and simplicity. Some of our greatest classics were written from this point of view: *Robinson Crusoe, Huckleberry Finn* and *Treasure Island*.

To examine another quite different area of fiction, it's doubtful that Philip Marlowe would have been so complex and fascinating if Raymond Chandler had chosen to tell us his thoughts about private eye ethics rather than letting us hear them directly from Marlowe.

B. THIRD PERSON

Third person has the advantages of breadth. No first person narrative can hope to attain the scope of, say, *War and Peace* or *Moby Dick* or on a more commercial level, *Gone With the Wind*. This fly-on-the-wall method allows the writer to get into characters and situations to a depth rarely achieved in first person. Even when used by such masters as Defoe, Twain and Stevenson the writer can never enter the minds of subsidiary characters like Man Friday, Jim and Ben Gunn. And one can only view Crusoe's island, the Mississippi and Treasure Island through the main characters' eyes.

For a long novel involving many changes of setting with a huge cast, third person is best. For shorter novels and stories involving one setting and three or four major characters, first person is faster, and generally less difficult and more rewarding for the writer.

Listen to this advice from agent Scott Meredith in his fine book, *Writing To Sell*:

> "About the only time first-person storytelling is preferable to third-person is when the entire fact that the script is being told in the lead character's own idiom or unusual manner characterizes him more deftly or accurately. You can, for example, build up a character as tough or ruthless by his actions and conversation in third-person telling but sometimes the fact that he does *all* the talking

in a first-person script—so that, in effect, you're characterizing him with every line—will accomplish this more strongly. In almost all other cases, the third-person method is preferable."

Remember, far more third-person novels are bought and published than first-person ones.

C. OTHER

The other forms—second person and stories told in the plural—are tricky types which you'll see once in a green moon. Do them as often. Likewise for stories told in letter or telegram form.

26

POSTPARTUM

*"Finishing a book is just like you took a child out
in the yard and shot it."*

— Truman Capote

All the writers we knew and know have felt a terrible void
after finishing a book and sometimes after a story, too.

There's only one antidote: starting another story or
novel.

Before we end this section we want to let you, the aspiring writer, understand a few things.

First, becoming a professional writer is not easy. A
recent article in *Harper's* magazine says that the percentage of American households in which no books are bought
is 60.

Also we agree with Donald Newlove, who says in his book *First Paragraphs* (St. Martins Press):

> Writing can get you fed to a lion whose teeth draw your whole face into its foul wet breath and cut your skull with knives. There's no soft way to put this. A black hole swallows you up. Willpower's no help. Getting in print is like beating cancer but losing a lung, staying in print is hopeless. Your best work goes begging. Short stuff has no market. Whatever checks show up—late—you brace at once against the toppling rent and insurance. One by one, your kids in print are pulped, your manuscript trunk feels full of backbreaking author chain, or bodies awaiting Christ, your work's shot down monthly by editors, agents give up on you, and you feed off whatever you write today.

However he also goes on to say:

> That's the big loaf that never dies. Today's paragraph comes, a word from the heart of the universe, and shines in the darkness, unquenched.
> And you ask for power, wisdom, and love as you make the anvil sing.

Yes indeed.

We also believe the following from Lawrence Block *On Writing Fiction* (*Writer's Digest* Books):

I used to think that talent, if present, was always visible. If a person showed you a piece of writing that was utterly without merit, writing in which not a shred of talent was evident, I figured you could tell him to give up, that he could never be a writer.

I have learned different. I have seen enough examples of writers who at one stage displayed absolutely no talent, and who went on to demonstrate abundant talent at a later date, to change my view of what talent is. I find myself coming increasingly to the belief that everyone has talent. For some it lies close to the surface, so that it takes little effort or will to bring it out into the open. For others, it lies deep within, accessible only to those who . . . want it badly enough.

In the end we are inclined to stand with this statement:

"If we had to say what writing is, we would define it essentially as an act of courage."

— Cynthia Ozick

So have fun:

"What release to write so that one forgets oneself, forgets one's companion, forgets where one is or what one is going to do next—to be drenched in sleep or in the sea. Pencils and pads and curling blue sheets alive with letters heap up on the desk."

— Anne Morrow Lindbergh

And when you read what you've written try to remember:

"I think I did pretty well, considering I started out with nothing but a bunch of blank paper."

— Steve Martin

And when life gets in the way, take a lesson from a master:

After Michelangelo died, someone found in his studio a piece of paper on which he had written a note to his apprentice, in the handwriting of his old age: "Draw, Antonio, draw, Antonio, draw and do not waste time."

Part III

MARKETING

SHORT STORIES

27

GUIDELINES

Recently we found ourselves in one of those antique shops which sell copies of magazines, some of which go back to the 1920s.

While thumbing through *Vanity Fair, Colliers* and *Saturday Evening Post* we were astounded to see that each contained six or eight stories per issue, some of which were five, even ten thousand words long!

Nowadays, even those "slick" or commercial magazines that can be called stalwarts of fiction (e.g. *Redbook*) only carry one story an issue, not exceeding fifteen hundred words.

McCall's and *Mademoiselle* have long stopped publishing fiction. *Redbook* says: "Of the 20,000 unsolicited manuscripts that we receive annually, we buy about 20 or more stories a year." *Good Housekeeping* says: "We get 1,500 unsolicited manuscripts per month—including poetry; a freelancer's odds are overwhelming—but we do look at all submissions."

The sad truth is that Americans read much less than we once did, and many prefer nonfiction to fiction.

For example, the number of collections of short stories published by commercial houses is minuscule, and most of these are by best-selling writers.

That is the bad news. The encouraging news is that there have never been so many literary or "little" magazines who publish fiction, nor as many regional magazines and newspapers who publish short stories.

While it's true that a handful of writers can expect to earn a living writing short stories, as Scott Fitzgerald did in the 1920s, there are many more opportunities to get stories published if one doesn't need the money.

The International Directory of Little Magazines and Small Presses (Dustbooks, P.O. Box 100, Paradise, California 95969), the *Writer's Market* and *Novel and Short Story Writer's Market* (c/o *Writer's Digest* Books) are all excellent sources.

Every mass circulation magazine has free guidelines that one can obtain by request. These spell out taboos, length, restrictions and slant.

There is a marvelous book containing over 260 reproductions of "periodical editors' instructions" called *Fiction Writers Guidelines* published by McFarland & Company, Inc. (Box 600, Jefferson, North Carolina 28640).

In this excerpt from compiler and editor Judy Mandell's preface, one can see how useful a tool this book is.

Fiction Writers Guidelines, Second Edition, includes guidelines prepared by the editors of 263 magazines that publish fiction as well as comments from the editors of 9 additional publications that do not provide guidelines but do accept freelance contributions. This enlarged and updated second edition is a useful tool for novice and professional writers, students, scholars, and teachers of writing. It also provides a behind-the-scenes look at the editorial policies of magazines.

The compilation includes magazines found on large and comprehensive newsstands, periodicals sold on a subscription basis only, and literary magazines. The little literaries may serve as springboards for novice writers, while the larger, more prestigious magazines provide outlets for well established writers of fiction.

All fiction writers will find this compilation of guidelines useful. This book should help the writer who is uncertain about where to send the work he or she has written as well as the writer who already has the periodical in mind but doesn't quite know the requirements of the publication. Even if the author has thoroughly read the magazine and thinks he's figured out its tone, style, content, and readership, he's better off knowing exactly what the magazine's editors have to say about what they want from freelancers.

SOME EXAMPLES OF GUIDELINES

Cosmopolitan

Cosmopolitan, 224 West 57th Street, New York, New York 10019

Helen Gurley Brown, Editor. Issued monthly, $1.95 a copy, $24.00 a year.

Nonfiction: Roberta Ashley, Executive Editor. Magazine aims at young career women. All nonfiction should tell these readers 1) how they can improve their lives, 2) better enjoy their lives, and 3) live better lives. Within this sphere, articles can be of the widest range, from celebrity profiles to psychological/sociological pieces of humor. Crisp, incisive, entertaining writing is a must, with a heavy emphasis on reader involvement. Full-length articles should be about 5,000 words, features 1,000 to 3,000 words. Payment for full-lengthers usually varies from $750 to $1500, but this is open to negotiation. Payment for features is proportionately less.

Fiction: Betty Kelly, Fiction and Books Editor. Stories must have solid upbeat plots, and sharp characterization. They should focus on contemporary man-woman relationships. Sophisticated handling and sensitive approach is a must, and female protagonists are preferred since our readers most easily identify with them. Short-shorts range from 1,500 words to 3,000 words; Short-stories from 4,000 to 6,000 words. Payment is $1,000 and up for short stories, from $300 to $600 for short-shorts. *Previously published* serious novels and mystery and suspense novels are sought for condensing and excerpting; payment here is open to negotiation, with the author's agent or hardcover publisher.

PLEASE ENCLOSE A SELF-ADDRESSED STAMPED ENVELOPE OR YOUR SUBMISSION CANNOT BE RETURNED.

Ladies' Home Journal

Thank you for your letter of inquiry regarding writer's guidelines for *Ladies' Home Journal.*

In order not to restrict the originality of our material, we have not set content guidelines for the *Journal.* The best advice that we can give you is to do a little research of your own. Read the *Journal* from cover to cover. In this manner you will become familiar with our fiction and editorial content and at the same time be able to tailor your work to our needs.

Because the volume of unsolicited material has become overwhelming, we ask that fiction be submitted through an agent who knows our publishing needs. We regret that this is the case, but a shortage of time and staff makes the careful consideration of all unsolicited manuscripts impossible.

Otherwise, please remember that we have a lead time of at least three months, and seasonal material is usually considered four or five months in advance. Also, always include a self-addressed, stamped envelope and a list of credits or a resumé if you have been published before. *The Journal* assumes no responsibility for unsolicited material.

Thank you for your interest.

Prairie Schooner

Prairie Schooner Writer's Guidelines

Thank you for your interest in our magazine. *Prairie Schooner* publishes short stories, poems, interviews, imaginative essays of general interest, and reviews of current books of poetry and fiction. Scholarly articles requiring footnote references should be submitted to journals of literary scholarship.

Prairie Schooner's intention is to publish the best writing available, both from beginning and established writers. In our sixty-five years of continuous publication, we have printed the work of Eudora Welty, Mari Sandoz, Jessamyn West, Randall Jarrell, Loren Eiseley, Diane Wakoski and others.

All submissions to *Prairie Schooner* should be typed double-spaced on one side of the paper only. Number pages consecutively and use margins of at least one inch. Be sure to put your last name on each page of the manuscript. A self-addressed envelope, with adequate return postage on it, must accompany the submission. *Prairie Schooner* does not read simultaneous submissions. Please allow three months for a reply.

We encourage you to read *Prairie Schooner*. Sample copies of previous issues are available for $2.00 and current issues are $4.00 each. Subscription prices are as follows: $15 for one year, $28 for two years, and $39 for three years. To subscribe or order a copy, fill out the form below and send it and your payment to the address above.

— the Editors

The Antioch Review

The best answer we can give on inquiries relating to what kind of material the *Antioch Review* uses is, "read the magazine." Look through a few representative issues for an idea of subjects, treatment, lengths of articles, and stories we have used; it will be far more rewarding than any general theories we might try to formulate.

Unfortunately, we cannot honor requests for free sample copies. The *Review* is expensive to produce and operates on a precarious financial margin. If copies are not available at your local newsstand or library, we will be happy to send you a back issue for $5.00, which includes postage and handling.

Articles: Our audience is the educated citizen, often a professional person, who is interested in matters beyond his field of special activity. With few exceptions, our subjects cover most of the range of the social sciences and humanities. Our approach tries to steer a middle course between the scholar speaking exclusively to other scholars in his field, and a workday journalist appealing to a broad popular audience; both these approaches have their own journals and audiences. We try for the interpretative essay on a topic of current importance, drawing on scholarly material for its substance and appealing to the intellectual and social concerns of our readers. We are also interested in reviving the moribund art of literary journalism.

Fiction: We seldom publish more than three short stories in each issue. Although the new writer as well as the previously published author is welcome, it is the story that counts, a story worthy of the serious attention of an intelligent reader, a story that is compelling, written with distinction. Only rarely do we publish translations of well known or new foreign writers; a chapter of a novel is welcome only if it can be read complete in itself as a short story.

Poetry: Like fiction, we get far more poetry than we can possibly accept, and the competition is keen. Here, where form and content are so inseparable and reaction is so personal, it is difficult to state requirements or limitations. Studying recent issues of the *Review* should be helpful. No "light" or inspirational verse. We do not read poetry manuscripts in the summer. Do not send any between May 15 and September 1.

Reviews: We do not publish unsolicited book reviews and very seldom do we publish essays on literary problems or on the cannons of significant contemporary writers. The editors and their associates regularly prepare a section of short book evaluations, selectively treating recent publications.

ACM

Guidelines for Contributors

Subscriptions: $15/yr, 2 issues
Sample copy: $5

Fiction: Double spaced, typed, no length limit. But please know the magazine. Fantasy, Mystery, Sci-fi, other genre *very* unlikely.

Poetry: Single or double spaced, typed, no length limit. Again, know the magazine. We want the freshest, best contemporary poetry, meaning words that *mean* in the world. We're mostly bored with sentimental hothouse melancholia of too much contemporary poetry. Mostly free verse, no "inspirational," or religious.

Essays/Reviews: On literary-related subjects, we're interested; but no academic documents to add to your tenure file, please.

Etc: Pound's still right: make it new.

ALWAYS ENCLOSE SELF-ADDRESSED STAMPED ENVELOPE FOR REPLY

Simultaneous submissions: Do it. We all take too long and don't expect you to wait forever. BUT we do expect to be notified immediately when work has been accepted elsewhere and is therefore withdrawn from *ACM* consideration. We understand that *ACM* appearance is the first of any work submitted to us, unless we are notified first.

Replies/Acceptance/Payments: Like most literary magazines, we're a nonprofit, struggling operation which can't afford to pay much—a barely token honorarium of $5–$10/poems and reviews, $25–$50/fiction and other longer prose. We try to send notice within 8 weeks, though it sometimes takes longer—and usually the longer the wait, the more tempted we are by the piece. If we accept the work, we understand you grant us first serial rights; all subsequent rights are yours, though we expect any future publication to carry acknowledgment that the work first appeared in *ACM*.

The Atlantic

The Atlantic is always interested in poetry, fiction, and articles of the highest quality. A general familiarity with what we have published in the past is the best guide to our needs and preferences. Simply send your manuscript—typewritten, double spaced, and accompanied by a return envelope and postage—to this address. Thank you for your interest.

— THE EDITORS

Seventeen

Fiction Guidelines

Seventeen publishes one 1000 to 4000-word story each month and pays $700 to $2000 on acceptance for first-time rights. We welcome stories that are relevant to adolescents and their experience, fiction that somehow touches contemporary young adult life. We are looking for submissions that will be accessible and appealing to our readers (ages 13–21), as well as challenging and inspiring. In essence, we want stories that possess the quality and integrity of today's best literary short fiction.

Winner of the 1984 National Magazine Award for outstanding editorial achievement in fiction, *Seventeen* has published such distinguished writers as Anne Tyler, Lorrie Moore, Michael Dorris, Joyce Carol Oates, Joy Williams, Amy Tan, and Margaret Atwood.

All submissions must be typed double-spaced and accompanied by a self-addressed, stamped envelope (SASE) large enough to accommodate the manuscript. Manuscripts without SASEs will not be returned. Address all submissions to the Fiction Editor, *Seventeen,* 850 Third Avenue, New York, New York 10022. We read all submissions and try to respond within eight weeks. We regret that we cannot offer individual comments or criticism.

We also run an annual fiction contest. Rules for the contest are published each year in either our October or November issue.

We strongly recommend reading the magazine before submitting your work.

28

SUBMISSION FORM

A. WORD COUNTS

The most accurate way to determine word count is to count the exact number of words. For those fortunate enough to own a word processor or computer, this is no problem. For the rest, here's how to estimate wordage.

Count the exact number of words on the first three pages of your manuscript (in manuscripts of 25 or fewer pages), divide total by three, and multiply the result by the number of pages. Carry the total to the nearest 100 words. (Note: Every word counts. The word "a" counts as a word. Abbreviated words count as one word.) For example, say you have a 12-page manuscript with totals of 182, 316 and 289 words on the first three pages. Divide your total of 787 by 3 to get 262. Now multiply 262 x 12 pages and you get

3,144. Your approximate wordage, therefore, will be 3,100 words. On manuscripts of more than 25 pages, count five pages instead of three, then follow the same process, dividing by 5 instead of 3.

Another way, less accurate but faster and quite sufficient, is to take the total number of every word big or small on two typed pages, divide by 2 and multiply by the number of pages.

B. WHY YOU SHOULD PRESS FOR CURRENT FICTION EDITOR'S NAME

Editors change jobs frequently. So even if you've read the editor's name in the latest issue of *Writer's Market* it's quite possible that editor has left since publication. A perfect example can be found in the previous chapter, under the *Cosmopolitan* listing. Helen Gurley Brown is no longer the editor but is still listed as such.

For this reason, the first step in querying a magazine is to address your letter to the correct editor and the right department.

Queries that are simply marked "Editor" may as well have a big red stamp across the envelope that says "amateur." Think about it—do you consider mail addressed "Current Resident" important?

You can often determine who the contact editor is by glancing at the magazine's masthead, the listing of its editorial staff. Title can be vague, though; for example,

"Associate Editor" or "Senior Editor" tells you nothing about the subjects these people specialize in. Furthermore, editors sometimes will have taken on new responsibilities months before the masthead reflects that change. A phone call to the magazine's editorial department will give you the information you need.

Once you've got the right name, be sure you spell it correctly.

C. MULTIPLE SUBMISSIONS, OR "WHAT IF MORE THAN ONE MAGAZINE WANTS MY STORY?"

Most magazines take an average of two months to respond to a submission, sometimes even longer.

If you were to submit to only one at a time merely six submissions would take one year's waiting time. Having more than one magazine wanting to publish your story is not exactly akin to having an itch during an MRI. Simply choose the publisher you'd most prefer being published by and tell the other you've made a mistake. With the odds stacked so astonishingly against you, you must dare to burn a bridge now and then.

D. COVER LETTERS

If there's one thing editors hate it's a cutesy, overly familiar cover letter. The kind that begins: "I'm sure you're very

busy and no doubt you've got a desk piled high with unsolicited manuscripts . . ."

Just get down to business. The editor doesn't care if
you've "just completed" it, how long you spent bleeding
over it and *definitely* not who already turned it down.

And please don't say how "topical" the story is or what
a great movie it would make.

Limit your sales pitch to any prior credits (fiction publication in literary or general circulation magazines or newspapers). Do not list nonfiction publications. If you lack
fiction credentials don't apologize—just don't mention it.

In sum, hold the hard sell. The point of a cover letter is
to *briefly* introduce yourself and the work, not influence the
sale. For that the story must speak for itself.

E. COLLECTIONS OF SHORT STORIES

Collections are difficult to market simply because readers
don't read collections any more avidly than they do short
stories. Best bet here is the university presses like the ones
at Indiana, Illinois and Louisiana State University.

F. HOW MANY REJECTS BEFORE I QUIT?

Rejects come in an ascending hierarchy: form rejections,
form rejections with scribble notes on them ("We'd like to
see more of your work" "Sorry—but this came close"),

critiques, letters saying the editor is willing to look at the story again after revision.

Track how many of each type of rejection you receive. What is the proportion of rejection slips to personalized ones, of form letters to individual notes?

But there are other questions you might ask. Are you the type who usually gets discouraged too soon in whatever you're doing? Are you the kind who has hurt yourself in the past by thrashing dead horses?

The most idealistic answer to "When should I quit?" is *never*. Keep at it, and usually the story or novel will eventually be published.

But there are few professionals who don't have a story or novel somewhere in their trunk they could never sell.

Ultimately your answer will probably have to do more with how you deal psychologically with rejection than any marketing formula.

One thing, however, is sure: If you're continuing to write other stories or novels while you're being rejected the pain won't be as bad. The more fiction you write the more you'll improve your chances. You'll better your chances even more by increasing the number of stories you're submitting.

When you get discouraged, try to remember that Gene Wolfe, author of the highly acclaimed *Book of the New Sun* wrote stories steadily for eight years before one sold.

And if you believe you're too old, think of Jean Auel who began her enormously successful prehistoric novels a few months after her fortieth birthday, after raising five children. Or Helen Hoover Santmeyer who published the bestselling . . . *And Ladies of the Club* in her eighties while she was in a nursing home.

If you're still on the floor from your rejects, we suggest you get a copy of *Rotten Reviews*, a collection of excerpts from scathing reviews of some of the most immortal writers who ever lived. This diamond from Pushcart Press was edited by Bill Henderson who edits *The Pushcart Prize*. Here is a smattering of delicious examples:

A MIDSUMMER NIGHT'S DREAM
William Shakespeare
Performed in London, 1662

The most insipid, ridiculous play that I ever saw in my life.

— Samuel Pepys,
Diary

OTHELLO
William Shakespeare
1604

Pure melodrama. There is not a touch of characterization that goes below the skin.

— George Bernard Shaw,
Saturday Review 1897

ANNA KARENINA
Leo Tolstoi
1877

Sentimental rubbish ... Show me one page that contains an idea.

— The Odessa Courier

MOBY DICK
Herman Melville
1851

An ill-compounded mixture of romance and matter of fact ... Mr. Melville has to thank himself only if his errors and his heroics are flung aside by the general reader as so much trash belonging to the worst school of bedlam literature—since he seems not so much unable to learn as disdainful of learning the craft of an artist.

— Athenaeum

MADAME BOVARY
Gustave Flaubert
1857

Monsieur Flaubert is not a writer.

— Le Figaro

A PASSAGE TO INDIA
E.M. Forester
1942

Spiritually it is lacking in insight.

— Blanche Watson,
The World Tomorrow

On
Jane Austen

I am at a loss to understand why people hold Miss Austen's novels at so high a rate, which seem to me vulgar in tone, sterile in artistic invention, imprisoned in the wretched conventions of English society, without genius, wit, or knowledge of the world. Never was life so pinched and narrow. The one problem in the mind of the writer . . . is marriageableness . . . Suicide is more respectable.

— Ralph Waldo Emerson,
Journal 1861

YOUTH and HEART OF DARKNESS
Joseph Conrad
1902

It would be useless to pretend that they can be very widely read.

— *Manchester Guardian*

A TALE OF TWO CITIES
Charles Dickens
1859

Last winter I forced myself through his *Tale of Two Cities*. It was a sheer dead pull from start to finish. It all seemed so insincere, such a transparent make-believe, a mere piece of acting.

— John Burroughs,
Century Magazine 1897

THE ADVENTURES OF HUCKLEBERRY FINN
Mark Twain
1884

A gross trifling with every fine feeling . . . Mr. Clemens has no reliable sense of propriety.

Springfield Republican

ULYSSES
James Joyce
1922

I finished Ulysses and think it is a misfire . . . The book is diffuse. It is brackish. It is pretentious. It is underbred, not only in the obvious but in the literary sense. A first rate writer, I mean, respects writing too much to be tricky.

— Virginia Woolf,
in her diary

ALICE IN WONDERLAND
Lewis Carroll
1865

We fancy that any real child might be more puzzled than enchanted by this stiff, overwrought story.

— Children's Books

On
Henry James

It is becoming painfully evident that Mr. James has written himself out as far as the international novel is concerned, and probably as far as any kind of novel-writing is concerned.

— William Morton Payne,
The Dial 1884

(still to come from James were *The Bostonians, The Turn of the Screw, The Ambassadors* and others — Ed.)

ABSALOM, ABSALOM!
William Faulkner
1936

The final blowup of what was once a remarkable, if minor, talent.

— Clifton Fadiman,
The New Yorker

THE GREAT GATSBY
F. Scott Fitzgerald
1925

Mr. F. Scott Fitzgerald deserves a good shaking
... *The Great Gatsby* is an absurd story, whether
considered as romance, melodrama, or plain
record of New York high life.

— Saturday Review of Literature

THE SUN ALSO RISES
Ernest Hemingway
1926

His characters are as shallow as the saucers in
which they stack their daily emotions, and
instead of interpreting his material—or even challenging it—he has been content merely to make a
carbon copy of a not particular significant surface
life of Paris.

— The Dial

THE CATCHER IN THE RYE
J.D. Salinger
1951

Recent war novels have accustomed us all to ugly
words and images, but from the mouths of the
very young and protected they sound peculiarly
offensive ... the ear refuses to believe.

— New York Herald Tribune Book Review

NOVELS

Commercial publishers, small
presses, sources of information,
requirements of publishers

29

Twenty years ago, an aspiring novelist could send his novel to any one of the major publishers in New York City and assume he would be read—in time. The system was called "over the transom." Manuscripts that came in that way went in the "slush pile."

Readers at a publishing house, barely out of college, would read unsolicited material. Once in a great while one of these readers would tug the sleeve of an editor, and this would then result in a sale. One such victor from the slush pile was Judith Guest's *Ordinary People* which went on to be a bestseller and was adapted into an Academy Award winning motion picture.

Nowadays the slush pile is all but gone. Major publishers come right out and say in print they don't read unsolicited manuscripts. But there are exceptions. Sandy

McDonald, a submission reviewer for a "major independent publisher" says, "Of the five thousand-odd proposals I paw through yearly, only one is likely to make it all the way to book world."

We strongly recommend that an aspiring novelist do one of two things: Find an agent, or send his work to small presses.

The major publishers assume that if you don't have an agent you can't get one.

They also assume that dealing directly with an amateur is setting themselves up for plenty of aggravation. Most small publishers are accustomed to dealing with writers directly.

Sources of information about the requirements of publishing may be found in the same books we recommend for the marketing of short stories.

GUIDELINES

1. By all means, multiple submit.

2. The amount of rejects before-you-quit question can be answered identically for novel marketing as well as short stories. *Gone With the Wind* was rejected over 30 times before it connected. The decision is up to you.

3. Try marketing your novel in hardcover markets first. If you don't you're automatically eliminating your chances of a follow-up mass market sale. Book

reviewers are also still prejudiced against paper-
backs, and Hollywood often snubs its nose at a
paper cover.

4. There are only a few paperback houses, and these
are constantly being sold or bought. Therefore,
phone before you submit.

5. A trade paperback is a hardcover-size book with
paper covers, though some houses, like Vintage, do
literary books in soft cover.

6. Midlist books are ones with potential but which
aren't expected to become bestsellers. Tony
Hillerman's books were midlist not long ago before
he hit it big. With few exceptions, most writers'
novels start off being mid- or low-list with minimum
promotion. In the past, publishers accepted this
truism. They'd groom their writers, believing in time
they'd develop a readership. While this is still partly
true, the current emphasis on blockbuster first novels
is making it ever tougher for other new novelists.

7. Whenever you can afford to submit your entire
novel, don't waste time submitting a portion and an
outline. Publishers seldom sign up unfinished novels
from unpublished novelists.

8. Response time for novels can vary from say, three
weeks to three months. Don't hesitate to query after a
normal wait.

9. Cover letters. Basically, follow the same philosophy
as for short stories. However, if you've actually

worked on Arabian oil rigs for your Middle Eastern thriller, by all means mention it. You might say what inspired you to write the novel. But don't be preachy, and spare the editor an endless, elaborate outline. Be straightforward, sincere and brief.

AGENTS

30

Many say it's more important to get an agent today than a publisher. We're not sure if this is true, but we do know that agents are becoming essential to a novelist. They're needed to sell the writer's work. Today publishing houses are having a difficult time so they are downsizing. Thus ex-editors frequently become agents—often good ones. As these new agents have ties with the remaining editors and the working editors trust their judgment, their clients get better treatment than unsolicited manuscripts.

A. WHAT NOT TO EXPECT

Agents are not there to 1) lend you money, 2) teach you how to write, 3) listen to your angst about the dwindling rate of fiction being read or published, 4) be accessible when they leave their office, 5) take badgering calls when you phone asking for reports on submissions.

B. WHAT TO EXPECT

Agents are expected to 1) inform you of every offer by a publisher, 2) to leave the acceptance of a low contract offer or a rewrite up to you, 3) furnish you with copies of your rejects every quarter.

C. WHAT TO LOOK FOR

Anyone can call himself an agent and stick manuscripts in envelopes to editors whose names he looks up in *Literary Market Place* or a book listing all agents. A good agent knows the particular tastes and editorial needs of many editors and publishers. He has resources. He will phone a specific editor for a specific novel and say, "Barbra, this one's for you."

A true agent who believes in a client's work will literally never stop trying to sell it. He'll exhaust every publishing house, and then go back to different editors at the same houses.

D. PROFESSIONALISM

Remember, you're seeking an agent, not shopping for a friend or confidant. This is a business relationship. It should certainly be cordial, even friendly, and a few writer/agent relationships have been intimate. But the safest relationship to have with an agent is a businesslike one.

E. SPECIALIZING

Besides tenacity, look for an agent who specializes in the particular kind of novel you write—literary, mainstream, science fiction, mystery, romance, western, horror, etc. This kind of agent will invariably have good contacts among those editors who specialize in your particular kind of novel.

F. READING FEES AND UP FRONT EXPENSES

Twenty years ago, an agent charging a reader's fee was considered a charlatan. Anyone charging a "marketing" fee in advance for postage, copies and phone calls was considered little short of a mugger.

Today, there are many more agents who do charge reading fees. And more and more agents are charging marketing fees in advance.

Let's examine how this evolved. When many publishers began refusing to read anything but manuscripts sent in by agents, the onus of reading most of the novels was left to the agents. The agents were, and still are not staffed to read that amount of material.

We work as editors with referrals from dozens of agents, most of whom receive hundreds of submissions per month.

If these agents were to hire qualified outside readers to read all their submissions they would have to find numerous bestsellers to offset this enormous investment in reader fees. The publishing houses passed their costs to the agents.

Faced with this financial burden, many agents closed their doors to new writers—unless existing clients recommend a new writer's work. So agents began to charge fees just to consider a manuscript. These fees range from a dollar per double-spaced page to several dollars a page, the average being about $1.50. This is certainly not an unreasonable amount when compared, for example, to a typing service charging a dollar a page to type a manuscript.

G. CONTRACTS—HOW LONG TO STAY MARRIED TO YOUR AGENT

In the past, agents rarely had contracts with writers. They felt that they didn't want to deal with clients who no longer wanted to be represented by them. However, as one famous agent put it to us: "I don't want to work with someone new who might leave before I even get back my investment in time and money."

This is a legitimate argument, and this particular agent certainly has done well for new writers. But you may be more comfortable with an agent who has to depend on his performance rather than a contract to hold his clients. If your agent has demonstrated that he's a tenacious marketer but hasn't sold your work or you're discouraged with the kind of advances he's getting you, you must make an honest appraisal of your writing skills and marketing. Good agents can't sell mundane books or get huge sums for mid-list ones.

H. WHERE TO FIND LISTS OF AGENTS

Writer's Market publishes a yearly book entitled *Guide to Literary Agents* which lists 500 agents who handle novels and short stories. These lists are divided into non-fee charging and fee-charging agents.

Also included is: a) how long an agent has been in business, b) how many clients he has, c) what percentage of books are fiction, d) reporting times on manuscripts, e) recent sales, f) terms, g) whether a writer's contract is offered, g) what writer's conferences are attended and "tips." If, for example, a tip reads: "Obtains new clients through recommendations" or "We're accepting only writers who have been published, don't waste time." However, if you have never been published, and the tip reads: "Obtains new clients through referrals and over the transom," this is a good lead for a newcomer.

Literary Market Place is another excellent publication that lists agents but with a limited amount of information.

I. HOW AND WHY CLIVE CUSSLER AND OUR FRIEND MARIE FORMED THEIR OWN LITERARY AGENCY

It's a little known secret that Clive Cussler formed a literary agency to market his own work.

Many years ago, frustrated with the fact that most agents wouldn't handle short stories except as an accommodation to successful novelists, a dear friend—Marie—decided to investigate being an agent herself.

She discovered that unlike say, barbers, literary agents are not required to have a license of any kind in New York (or any other state that she checked).

After a modest investment with a printer, and a pseudonym, our friend was armed with elegant ivory bond letterheads with raised lettering.

At that time, general circulation magazines were almost all opposed to multiple submissions. Marie searched out a typing service who used automated typewriters. The result was copies no editor could tell from the original.

Now known as the Mary T. Williams Agency, Marie submitted a short story to fifty general circulation and literary magazines.

In the end (four months later) her story had been accepted by three literary magazines.

Marie—acting as Mary T. Williams—told her second and third choices there had been a mistake in submission. Neither minded a bit.

We're not advocating that anyone form a literary agency to market their work. What we are saying is that it was tough out there then, and it's tougher now. One must study and work to write as best he can. Then he must market with the zeal of an evangelist. It's that, or become part of the dreadful statistics on rejection.

RECOMMENDED
BOOKS TO READ

CRAFT

Characters Make Your Story by Maren Elwood. Published by The Writer, Boston. This is an excellent book (now in paperback).

The Art of Dramatic Writing by Lajos Egri. Available in trade paperback. If you can't find it, try bookstores specializing in theater.

Narrative Technique by Thomas Uzell. Harcourt Brace.

Understanding Fiction by Cleanth Brooks, Jr. and Robert Penn Warren. F.S. Crofts.

Language in Action by S.I. Hayakawa. Available in paperback.

The Use and Misuse of Language by S.I. Hayakawa. Available in paperback.

Spider Spin Me a Web: Lawrence Block on Writing Fiction by Lawrence Block. *Writer's Digest* Books.

Handbook of Short Story Writing Volume I by Dickson and Smythe. *Writer's Digest* Books.

Handbook of Short Story Writing Volume II edited by Jean Fredette. *Writer's Digest* Books.

Elements of Style. Strunk & White.

A Glossary of Literary Terms. Holt, Rhinhard & Winston.

Writing Without Teachers by Peter Elbow. Oxford University Press. (For "Writing Blocks.")

How to Write Best Selling Fiction and *Writing Popular Fiction* by Dean Koontz. *Writer's Digest* Books.

The Name Game by Christian Anderson. Simon & Schuster.

Characters & Viewpoint by Orson Scott Card. *Writer's Digest* Books.

Dare to Be a Great Writer by Leonard Bishop. *Writer's Digest* Books.

The Basic Patterns of Plot by Norman. University of Oklahoma Press, 1959.

Fiction Is Folks by Robert Newton Peck. *Writer's Digest* Books.

The Art of Fiction by John Gardner. Alfred E. Knopf, 1984.

On Moral Fiction by John Gardner. Basic Books, 1978.

The Writer's Craft by John Hersey. Alfred E. Knopf, 1974.

Aspects of the Novel by E.M. Forster. Harcourt, Brace & World, 1954.

Professional Fiction Writing: A Practical Guide to Modern Techniques. The Writer, Inc., 1974.

Writing a Novel by John Braine. McGraw, 1975.

If I Can Write, You Can Write by Charlie Shedd. *Writer's Digest* Books.

Storycrafting by Paul Darcy Bowles. *Writer's Digest* Books.

Dialogue by Lewis Turco. *Writer's Digest.*

The Writer on His Art by Walter Allen. McGraw-Hill Book Co.

Writing in General and the Short Story in Particular. Houghton Mifflin, 1977.

One Way to Write Short Stories by Ben Nyberg. *Writer's Digest* Books.

Revision by Kit Reed. *Writer's Digest* Books.

The Craft of Fiction by William C. Knott. Reston Publishing Co., 1977.

The Lonely Voice: A Study of the Short Story by Frank O'Connor. World Publishing Co., 1963.

Plot by Ansen Dibble. *Writer's Digest* Books.

Writers at Work: The Paris Review Interviews by George Plimpton. Viking Press, 1967–1981.

Beyond Style: Mastering the Finer Points of Writing by Gary Provost. *Writer's Digest* Books.

Afterwards: Writers on Their Novels by Thomas McKormack, ed. Harper & Row.

Just Open a Vein by William Brohaugh. *Writer's Digest* Books.

The Thirty-Six Dramatic Situations by George Polti. Lucille Gray, trans. The Writer, Inc., 1921.

Becoming a Writer by Dorothea Brande. J.P. Tarcher, Inc., 1981.

On Writing: Critical Studies on Writing as an Art by Willa Cather. Alfred E. Knopf.

How to Write and Sell Your First Novel by Frances Spatz Leighton with Oscar Collier. *Writer's Digest* Books.

Writing to Sell by Scott Meredith. Harper & Row, 1974.

The Writer on Her Work by Janet Sternburg, ed. W.W. Norton, 1981.

The Living Novel and Later Appreciations by V.S. Pritchett. Random House, 1964.

Mystery and Manners by Flannery O'Connor. Farrar, Straus & Giroux, 1969.

The 29 Most Common Writing Mistakes and How to Avoid Them by Judy Delton. *Writer's Digest* Books.

The Basic Formulas of Fiction by Foster-Harris. University of Oklahoma Press, 1977.

The Story of a Novel by Thomas Wolfe. Scribner, 1936.

Getting the Words Right: How to Revise, Edit and Rewrite by Theodore A. Rees Cheney. *Writer's Digest* Books.

Writer's Encyclopedia by Kirk Polking. *Writer's Digest* Books.

The Craft of Interviewing by John Brady. Random House, 1977.

Bird by bird: Some Instructions on Writing and Life by Ann Lamott. Pantheon 1994.

The Joy of Writing Sex: A Guide For Fiction Writers by Elizabeth Benedict. Story Press, 1996.

WRITING AS A BUSINESS

How to Write Irresistible Query Letters by Lisa Collier. Writer's Digest Books.

A Practical Guide to Writing, Illustrating and Publishing. Quadrangle Books, 1976.

Revising Prose by Richard A. Lanham. Charles Scribner.

A Writer's Guide to Book Publishing. Ayer Press, 1981.

How to Get Your Book Published by Herbert W. Bell. *Writer's Digest Books.*

Writer's Market, ed. Writer's Digest Books, yearly.

What Is An Editor? by Dorothy Cummins. University of Chicago Press.

Max Perkins, Editor of Genius. Pocket Books, 1983.

The Blockbuster Complex: Conglomerates, Show Business and Book Publishing by Thomas Whiteside. Wesleyan University Press, Connecticut, 1981.

A Beginner's Guide to Getting Published by Kirk Polking. *Writer's Digest* Books.

How to Write with a Collaborator by Hal Bennet with Michael Larsen. *Writer's Digest* Books.

LMP Literary Market Place. R.R. Bowker and Co.

A Writer's Guide to Copyright by Caroline R. Herron. Poets and Writers, Inc., 1979.

Complete Handbook for Freelance Writers. Writer's Digest Books.

Profitable Part-Time/Full-Time Freelancing. Writer's Digest Books.

Writer's Guide to Publishing in the West by Frances Helpern. Pinnacle West, 1982.

RESEARCH

The Modern Researcher by Jacques Barzun. Harcourt, Brace, Jovanovich, 1985.

On Writing, Editing and Publishing by Jacques Barzun. University of Chicago Press, 1971.

Law and the Writer. Writer's Digest Books.

The Writer and His Markets. Frank Reynolds. Doubleday & Co., 1978.

Writer's Guide to Research by Lois Horowitz. *Writer's Digest* Books.

Information U.S.A. by Matthew Lesko. Penguin Books, 1986.

Ayer Directory of Publications. Ayer Press, 1981.

NEWSLETTERS, MAGAZINES, JOURNALS, ETC.

The Information Advisor, 14 Franklin Street, Rochester, NY 14604.

The Information Report, 2612 P Street, Washington, DC 20007.

ORGANIZATIONS

Special Libraries Associations. 1700 18th Street NW, Washington, DC 20009.

Information Industry Association, 555 New Jersey Avenue NW, Suite 800, Washington, DC 20001.

Some of these books may have to be ordered from book search companies, usually listed in newspapers and writer's magazines because (a) publishers have dropped them from their lists or (b) publishers have gone out of business or merged under other names. They will be well worth the extra effort.

We have omitted the dates on *Writer's Digest* Books, as writing or calling the company is relatively simple, and they have a large, still functioning list. (*Writer's Digest* Books, 1507 Dana Avenue, Cincinnati, OH 45207).

A writer I knew once told me,

> "After writing for 20 years I realized I couldn't write. But now I can't quit because I'm too successful."

— Anonymous

ABOUT THE AUTHORS

William Appel has published five novels: *Waterworld, Watcher Within, White Jaguar, Whisper ... He Might Hear You*, and *Widowmaker*. He's also published short stories. Bill's book reviews have appeared in *Publisher's Weekly, The Buffalo News*, and *The Calgary Herald*. He's written a monthly magazine column and a weekly newspaper column. Bill taught creative writing at Bard College and was formerly on the faculty at the *Writer's Digest* School's criticism service as well as its advanced short story and novel writing courses. He's a member of P.E.N. and Mystery Writers of America. Of *The Truth About Fiction Writing*, Bill says, "This book is about not only how to write fiction, but how to recognize and use professional techniques or "tricks" in nonfiction as well. Equally important is the explicitness about how to find an agent and get your book published."

Denise Sterrs has been a reader for Meteor Publishers. She was an instructor for the *Writer's Digest* Advanced Short Story and Novel Writing courses. She's worked for the Write Word Workshop as a developmental editor under independent contract and has been a contributing writer to various specialty publications. Denise is currently at work on a book entitled, *Demystifying the Publishing Process*, as well as co-authoring a monthly column with Bill Appel called, "The Doctors Are In" for *Writers' Journal*. Additionally, she is a member of the Editorial Freelancers Association.

Currently, Bill and Denise are literary "scouts" for several literary agents, publishers and producers as well as presiding over a book doctoring (editing) service called Edit Ink. They'd be delighted to answer any of your questions about writing or publishing. Write to Edit Ink, 172 Holtz Drive, Cheektowaga, New York 14225. Phone 716-626-4431, fax 626-4388.

INDEX